"Jared Wilson provides a stern warning against the *excesses* of pragmatic approaches to church growth while reminding us that if the power of the gospel is not driving our ministries, we may build a crowd, but we are not building a church."

Thom S. Rainer, President and CEO, LifeWay Christian Resources

"Jared Wilson paints a vivid picture of the grievous outcome of church centered on programmatic pragmatism instead of the life-changing gospel of Jesus Christ. His critical analysis and probing confrontation, coupled with his personal encounter with grace, has the potential to bring the church to her senses and usher her back to our Father's restorative embrace. *The Prodigal Church* is a desperately needed wake-up call."

Jeff Vanderstelt, Visionary Leader, Soma; Pastor, Doxa Church, Bellevue, Washington; author, *Saturate*

"*The Prodigal Church* is indeed a gentle manifesto against the status quo. Wilson writes with humility, urgency, and true pastoral concern for God's people. He pushes back against the consumerism and pragmatism so prevalent in twenty-first-century congregations, and points the church to something far superior—the gospel of Jesus Christ. All who love the local church will benefit from reading this book."

Jason K. Allen, President, Midwestern Baptist Theological Seminary and College

"Jared Wilson writes that we've forgotten "who the church is for." He rightly, and with a kind spirit, questions the status quo in this book. The church is not a consumer experience. It's not supposed to be a volunteer-draining, CEO-driven business. No, it's much bigger, better, and more beautiful than that."

Brant Hansen, CURE International; storyteller; radio host; author, *Unoffendable*

"Although I don't agree with all of the conclusions Jared comes to, he asks penetrating questions and lovingly ar— —as a man who deeply loves Jesus, the gospel, the church, and pastors. —— ——t he has written here will save some weary ┌ ┐ ike The Village Church a healthier plac

Matt Chandler, Lead Pastor, ' President, Acts 29 Church Pla.

The Prodigal Church

The Prodigal Church

A Gentle Manifesto against
the Status Quo

Jared C. Wilson

WHEATON, ILLINOIS

Trade paperback ISBN: 978-1-4335-4461-3
ePub ISBN: 978-1-4335-4464-4
PDF ISBN: 978-1-4335-4462-0
Mobipocket ISBN: 978-1-4335-4463-7

Library of Congress Cataloging-in-Publication Data
Wilson, Jared C., 1975–
   The prodigal church : a gentle manifesto against the status quo / Jared C. Wilson.
      pages cm
   Includes bibliographical references and index.
   ISBN 978-1-4335-4461-3 (tp)
1. Church. I. Title.
BV600.3.W567   2015
277.3'083—dc23   2014018550

Crossway is a publishing ministry of Good News Publishers.

VP		25	24	23	22	21	20	19	18	17	16	15
15	14	13	12	11	10	9	8	7	6	5	4	3	2	1

Contents

Introduction: The Parable of the Prodigal Church   9

1   What This Book Is Not   15

2   What If the System's Broken?   25

3   What Works?   47

4   The Bible Is Not an Instruction Manual   71

5   From Watching to Beholding   91

6   Biting Off More Than You Can Chew   121

7   Pastoring Hearts   139

8   A Way Forward   155

9   The Prodigal Church Comes Home   177

10   A Portrait of the Author as a Young Man   193

Conclusion: A Call to the Gospel Renaissance   219

Recommended Reading   221

General Index   223

Scripture Index   229

Introduction

The Parable of the Prodigal Church

Once upon a time, there was a church that loved God and loved people but had a difficult time showing it because the image they gave of God was rather one-dimensional and so the way they attempted to love people was also one-dimensional. The church believed in a holy God, a just God, a vengeful God, and so they preached wrath very well, pushing the hearts of all who darkened the church doors with the imminent foreboding of their eternal damnation.

They did their best to scare the hell out of people, and when that didn't work, they cried and pleaded and begged. Wretchedly urgent, the church regularly reminded its people of the dire importance of obedience to God, of being holy as God is holy. And the church grew vividly aware, year in and year out, of the "thou shalt nots" of the Bible. And they came back for more, because guilt can be a powerful motivator.

But guilt is not a very *enduring* motivator, so as time went on and people grew weary of the burden of the law laid so heavily upon them, they began to drift away. Some had begun to suspect this church's God was not quite love and that this God could never quite be pleased, so they stopped trying. But some kept trying, of course, fearful and diminished.

One day some brave soul gently suggested that the old way wasn't working. People could not be won by a God who seemed angry all the time, he reasoned, and in fact it made no sense to expect people to have interest in a God who didn't seem to care about their happiness. The God of the old way seemed so preoccupied with holy things that he did not care much for people's everyday lives. "Couldn't we make the way of the church more practical, more appealing?" this person asked. "The way we may see growth again," he reasoned, "is to deconstruct the old way, remove the old barriers, and reassert that God is love."

So, where once the church emphasized God's perfect holiness, now they emphasized his abundant love. Where once the church emphasized obedience, now they emphasized success. Where once the church emphasized sin, now they emphasized happiness. Where once the church focused on God's demands, now they emphasized man's specialness and abilities. "If we help people tap into their inner potential and remind them of how special they are," the church decided, "and if we highlight how God loves them no matter what, people will be interested in church again."

They changed the songs, the architecture, the style of dress. They took the crosses down, because they seemed too religious. It was a clean slate. And, lo and behold, people began to come to church again.

The church grew in attendance week by week and year by year. People came excited and exuberant. This was not their grandfather's church!

But as the years went by, the church noticed something. Little by little, they discovered that while some new people were discovering church for the first time, most who came to experience the new way of doing church were actually in recovery from the old way of doing church. And while helping wounded people recover is not a bad thing at all, the church began to discover that most of their people—new Christians and "old" Christians alike—were not growing very deep in their faith. The lack, it seemed to them, was of a more relevant way to apply their faith to everyday life.

So the church came up with some new ideas to help people grow. They changed traditional Sunday school to innovative small groups, outdated special music to contemporary video montages. In order to help people see God's Word in the world around them, they began applying Bible verses to songs on the radio and movies at the theater. The church continued deconstructing more things, making more things over. The church had—in their own estimation, cleverly—traded out the "don'ts" for "dos," but in the end, they discovered that even the regular dispensing of practical helps for victorious living wasn't having the desired effect. People certainly enjoyed the weekend experience now. But, day by day, they still seemed no closer to God than in that old way of doing church. In fact, though it scared them to admit it, people actually seemed *less* interested in God than before.

For him who has ears to hear, this is the parable of the prodigal church.

For my own part I hate and distrust reactions not only in religion but in everything. Luther surely spoke very good sense when he compared humanity to a drunkard who, after falling off his horse on the right, falls off it next time on the left.

—C. S. Lewis, *The World's Last Night*

And he cautioned them, saying, "Watch out; beware of the leaven of the Pharisees and the leaven of Herod."

—Mark 8:15

1

What This Book Is Not

I dare you to read this book.

I don't dare you as someone who aims to make you mad (or sad), but as someone who himself has been dared to read things that have challenged his own assumptions and presumptions—which benefited him greatly in the long run. I just want to appeal to your desire as a leader to stretch and grow and be thoughtful and have firmer convictions than ever before. I just want to ask you some questions. I want to show you some things. I want you to consider some different lines of thinking, even if they end up leading you right back to affirming what you already thought.

If you don't like the book, return it and ask for a refund. Tell them I'm an idiot and these pages should line birdcages. But please give me the chance to earn your rejection. And if you will make the commitment to hear me out to the very end, I make these promises to you:

This Book Is Not a Rant

I'm pretty good at rants. Or at least, I feel pretty good when I rant. But this book will not be a grand venting. Who wants that? Not you. Not me. We've all had enough yelling in the Christian world, I think, or at least enough yelling about things that don't need yelling about.

I don't know about you, but I've got LOUD NOISES fatigue. When someone who disagrees with me thinks the only way to convince me is to trigger the All Caps button and lay heavy hands on the Exclamation Point key, I tune them out right-quick.

When I came up with the idea for this book, it began as an extension of things I've been thinking, writing, and preaching about for nearly ten years now, but this project is really the culmination of twenty years of life and ministry. I'm not writing purely from theory but from experience. But I also knew that some of the ways I've written about issues related to church models and methodology in the past would not be suitable for this book. Not because those previous ways were wrong, necessarily, but because they were often for different audiences, perhaps too often for the already convinced. Like many of you, I have that "spiritual gift" of sarcasm, but too often that kind of humor is used in harmful, cutting ways, in ways that are counterproductive. Like lots of people, I can too often vent my frustrations rather than plead my case. I want to take the Bible seriously when it says that venting is foolish (Prov. 29:11).

There's definitely a place for harsh words. We see them used in a variety of ways in the Bible, including to correct wrong belief and wrong action. But what I want you to read here isn't intended as a rebuke. I don't want to appall you; I want to appeal to you. I won't snip at you or nag you. I might *pester* you, but I definitely don't want to pick on you.

I'm also not writing this book to preach to the choir, which is all that ranting really ends up accomplishing. Preaching to the choir can be fine and good (the choir needs the preaching, too), but I know that if we expect others to not just hear what we're saying but also to actually *consider* it, we have to be kind, respectful, and affirming of all that we can affirm. So I won't lie and say this isn't a manifesto. It is. But hopefully it will be a gentle one. You can be the judge of whether I succeed or not.

This Book Is Not an Argument for a Traditional Church

You may think I want to sell you on a particular way of doing church. I do. I absolutely do. But I hope you will relax as it pertains to music styles, clothing styles, or almost any other kinds of styles, because this isn't that kind of book.

Many times, when a person complains about the so-called "attractional church," people understandably assume that the person is arguing for a "traditional church" instead. If I complain about the superficiality of certain contemporary worship songs, the response can be something like, "So you think we should just sing hymns?" Hymns are great. More churches should sing them. But there's nothing intrinsically holy about old music. When someone argues that too much contemporary Christian music is superficial or theologically suspect, it is not a call to give up songwriting but a call to write better songs.

I was once part of a rather large church that fell apart. The elders had to dismiss the lead pastor for a variety of sins, including ongoing verbal abuse of numerous staff members. The pastor announced a public meeting, which I attended, to give his side of the story, part of which consisted of saying the elders had kicked him out because they wanted to make the church more traditional. This was not true at all, and most of us saw right through it. But the pastor knew it would gain some traction because many people in our church were there "in recovery" from bad experiences of legalism and lifelessness in traditional churches. Traditionalism had become a handy bogeyman.

There are all kinds of churches in the world, and there are good ones and bad ones among all those kinds. There are good traditional churches and bad ones. There are good contemporary churches and bad ones. But when, faced with critique, the contemporary church holds up an idea of the traditional church as boring or fundamentalist or backward, it is the cheapest kind of defensiveness and self-justification.

So in my critique, I hope this kind of response will be set aside. I am not asking anyone to give up their guitars or their coffee bars—just, perhaps, to reconsider what they do with them. This is not an argument for a more traditional church so much as it is an argument for a more biblical one.

This Book Is Not a Reactionary Rejection

It has been said that the prophets of one generation become the Pharisees of the next. Maybe that's true.

What we see in the cyclical nature of the church in the Western world is how each generation in some way rebels against the values and establishments of the generation before it. Some track this reactionary cycle through the generations of church models, as well. It is possible that the rise of the so-called "seeker church," with the primary influences of Willow Creek Community Church in Illinois and Saddleback Community Church in California, precipitated a reactionary movement of similar churches against the traditional—maybe fundamentalist—churches before them. Then my generation, often called Generation X, began to flirt with things like liturgy, creeds, more structured worship, even candles and incense. In response to the loosened-up church style of the Boomers, the Xers went further back than their fundamentalist grandparents even, and adopted some sort of merging of contemporary church with elements of high church formalism, seeking less relevance and more reverence. We might say the movement known as the emerging (or emergent) church came from this reaction.

Today the church world is a bit fractured, with tribes springing up all over the place. The mantle of the Boomers' "seeker church" has been passed through the "church growth" movement, on to a new phase in contemporary church styles predominant in the American megachurch movement. But we have to be careful there, because not all megachurches are created equal. There are very big traditional churches and very big contemporary churches. The bigness of a church is no indicator of its style or approach to worship. Similarly, the seeker church paradigm can be found in hundreds of smaller churches around the nation.

The emergent church seems to have fractured off from evangelicalism altogether. Although there are certainly evangelicals in the emergent church movement, as a stream of church life it seems to have found itself more at home within the denominational mainline, where religious and political liberalism are more common.

The tribe sometimes called the "neo-Reformed"—or alternately, the new Calvinists, the neo-Puritans, the "young, restless, and Reformed"—is another offshoot of the contemporary church that ran parallel to the emerging church for a time. Those of us who identify with the slightly larger tent we might call the "gospel-centered" movement would align more with the neo-Reformed, but there is plenty of variety denominationally and stylistically even in this group. Just get the Presbyterians and the Baptists talking about baptism, for instance, or the traditionally Reformed folks and the Acts29 Network gang talking about church music.

There is a beauty in all of this diversity. It is legalism when we place a burden on another local church body to look more like our own than Christ's. So in all this beauty lies a great danger, and the danger is this: assigning a level of spirituality according to one's stance on an open-handed theological issue—that is, important but nonessential issues that we hold more loosely than the essential tenets of orthodox Christianity, which of course we hold very tightly in a "closed hand." We must be very careful that our modes and models of church are sincere attempts to contextualize our common faith to our particular mission fields and communities. In this vein, it is just as narrow-minded to suggest that a traditional church is necessarily boring and legalistic as it is to suggest that a contemporary church is shallow and worldly.

We've got to get out of reactionary mode. When we find ourselves making particular transitions from one way of doing church to another, we have to be on guard against shaking a fist at those in the places we leave behind.

I have deep concerns about the current approach to what used to be called the seeker church, what some today may call the "attractional" church. I think there are some fundamental assumptions and instrumental decisions being made at the heart of this way of doing church that are not in step with the truth of the gospel. I am trying to be totally up front about that. But if you are committed to that approach, I do not question your faith. I do not question your love for Jesus. I know that you do what you do precisely because you do love Jesus and because you love the people Jesus loves and want to be about the business Jesus was about. I know you do what you do because lost people need to know Christ; your way of worship style and preaching style—your entire mode of "doing church"—comes from a desire to do what many churches have simply left undone for many, many years, which is to say, reveal the loving heart of God for those spiritually far from him. You want lost people to be saved and you want found people to walk more closely with him. I see that, and honor it.

I will tell you, in the final chapter, my own personal story of transition from the traditional church to the attractional church and then into another way. But you should know, ahead of time, that I invested in the attractional church because I shared its heart for the lost. I still have not rejected its primary aims. I simply come at those aims from another angle now. So this book isn't intended as a reactionary diatribe. You wouldn't read that. I wouldn't read that. So I won't write that.

I'm writing this book not as a reactionary rejection of what you do, but as a reaction to what God has done in the gospel.

I'm asking you to thoughtfully consider the different angle laid out in these pages. You may think this is much ado about nothing, that this kind of stuff is petty. But I ask you to consider this carefully. I simply want to suggest that, even if we agree on the goal we are trying to reach, if we are just one or two tiny degrees off, the further we go the further away we will be from our intended destination.

And while faithful Christians may disagree on church forms and the like—while we may, in love, differ on all manner of secondary doctrinal matters—could it not be that some of these secondary things we differ on have implications for how people receive and believe primary things? How we "do church" shapes the way people see God and his Son and his ways in the world. If you agree with that, it behooves us to constantly evaluate what shape our church is taking and what shape of Christian our church is making.

This Book Is a Call to Question Ourselves

Many of our strongest churches began when a group of visionary people began to question the way they'd always done things. The best missionary work begins with an evaluation of previous work in the same field. The strategy begins with asking, "What has been done before? How fruitful has it been? What changes, if any, ought we to make?"

The worst ministry work assumes that the old ways of doing things are the best ways simply because "that's the way it's always been done." You and I laugh at this idea when it comes up in our churches. When we're not laughing, we're weeping. Many a great ministry initiative has stalled out, many a necessary alteration in the way of doing church has stopped before it began, because influential voices have raised the objection merely of its newness. No pastor wants to hear, "That's not the way the previous pastor did it."

The problem is that all of us are susceptible to this kind of thinking, including those of us in cutting-edge churches. We get locked into our ways of doing things and end up ruling out any questions or objections. The new way becomes the old way after a while, and we ourselves won't give any quarter to any newer ways of thinking because our *old* new way has been working just fine, thanks. Do you see how that works?

But if you are in a successful contemporary church, you didn't get where you are by doing things the way they've always been done. (I'm appealing to your sense of innovation here, and your willingness to evaluate things.) What happens when the innovative, relevant, cutting-edge ways of doing church become the old way? How do you know, for instance, that the way has gotten old? How do you know when the measurements you're making don't tell the whole story?

Do you, for instance, allow anyone to suggest that, despite all appearances, perhaps the way things are being done isn't the best way they *could* be done?

So here's what this book is intended to be:

You and I are sitting down for coffee. Or a long breakfast, since this is a book, not a pamphlet. I ask you, as a friend, to hear me out. I have some concerns about the way you're doing church. You're on guard, because you're tired of rants, tired of legalistic whining, tired of reactionary diatribes. You just want to get on with God's mission. I want that too. But for this long breakfast, I ask you to put the guard down and let me speak to you as a friend. As one iron sharpening another.

In Mark 8, Jesus and his disciples are in their boat after he has miraculously fed the four thousand. The disciples, as always, are a few tacos short of a combo. Jesus had just performed this great miracle using bread, and they very soon after are wondering where they're going to get some bread. Jesus, as he often does, turns their doubts into a teachable moment. In verse 15, he says, "Watch out; beware of the leaven of the Pharisees and the leaven of Herod."

This appears to come out of left field. The disciples miss the point right away and continue wondering about where to get bread. They don't know it, but their missing the point is actually quite *on* point.

When Jesus says to beware of the leaven (yeast) of the Pharisees, he is referring to self-righteousness, what we often call legalism. But legalism doesn't always look like rigid fundamentalist hellfire-and-brimstone Captain Bringdowns. (We'll talk about this later.) The point is that self-righteousness is very subtle. Just a little can spread and take over. The same is true of the leaven of Herod, by which I take Jesus to mean, essentially, "worldliness."

The leaven of the Pharisees and the leaven of Herod appear on the surface to be opposite dangers. Pharisees are religious; Herod is irreligious. Pharisees are legalistic; Herod is licentious. These are the two extremes we sinners often find ourselves swinging between on the great spiritual pendulum of life. Because this is true, it is true that our churches tend to swing between these poles as well. And often we justify our own tendencies by in some way saying, "Well, at least we're not like *those* guys."

But, "A little leaven leavens the whole lump" (Gal. 5:9). If we give either legalism or license an inch, they will take a mile. This is why Jesus says to "beware" of them both. And he also says to beware of them both so that we won't think that a dose of one is the antidote to the poison of the other.

That is the way many have forged their church movements. We hope to flee legalism by "loosening up." Or we hope to repent of worldliness by "tightening up." Certainly we could all use some loosening and tightening in strategic places, but this is not what Jesus is teaching.

In Mark 8 he has just fed the four thousand. The disciples are still wondering where they will get bread. Jesus says to beware of the bread of the Pharisees and beware of the bread of Herod. Because he wants us to find our bread in him, to find in fact that he *is* our bread.

If Jesus is, as he claims to be, the bread of life, what implications might this have for the way we do church? I don't simply mean that we will want people to know Jesus—I'm assuming you and I both already want that. That's the whole purpose of your church. The issue is this: Is it possible that the way we communicate the bread of life has been compromised by one of these other leavens that ought not be there? Jesus says to beware of this happening, so we shouldn't simply take for granted that good intentions will rule the possibility out.

What if the way we communicate Jesus actually works against people trusting him? Could we consider that together?

For all of the evaluation we tend to inflict upon ourselves— from test marketing felt needs to measuring the participation of our churchgoers, from studying the demographics of our target mission fields to critiquing the level of excellence of what takes place on our stages—I hope we have never ruled out asking, "What if what we're doing isn't really what we're supposed to be doing?"

We should ask that. All of us.

2

What If the
System's Broken?

The attractional church movement might be said to have begun with the rise of the seeker church movement—Willow Creek in Illinois and Saddleback in California being the two biggest pace-setters—but it has grown out of that movement into a nice amalgamation with the church growth movement, the multisite church movement, and—oddly enough—some of the traits and strategies of the traveling revivalists of the '50s, '60s, and '70s.

I am intimately familiar with the attractional church model, having both worked on staff and served as a layperson in attractional churches, and having been an ardent student and apologist of the seeker church movement for years. (Torn between two loves, I even once canceled my subscription to *Modern Reformation* magazine because I thought they picked on seeker churches too much.) I'm not an expert on the attractional model, and am for all intents and purposes a (hopefully respectful) critic of the model now, but I do believe I know some things about this way to do and be church.

A definition of "attractional" would perhaps be something like this: a way of ministry that derives from the primary purpose of making Christianity appealing. By this definition, it would not be an exaggeration to say that the attractional church makes its primary aim in worship to get as many people through the doors of the church as possible so that they may hear what it means to have a relationship with Jesus Christ.

The attractional paradigm does not necessarily neglect those who already believe, however; it seeks to help believers experience a more practical way of following Jesus, trusting that such instruction will also meet the primary aim of reaching the lost—by showing the appeal of Christianity as relevant to their daily life.

Let's be clear: *These are noble aims.* They are good-hearted and well-intentioned. The genesis of the seeker/attractional movement addressed very real problems—namely, that church members were not reaching their unsaved neighbors, and the unsaved neighbors could not see how Christianity had any relevance for modern life. Seeker churches sought to address such problems with very practical solutions. They wanted to make the experience of church as comfortable and *comprehensible* as possible so that those untrained in insider church lingo and unfamiliar with the Bible would see how utterly practical Christianity is. The goal, as we used to say, was to remove every stumbling block but the cross from between the lost and Jesus.

When I first read *Rediscovering Church* by Lynne and Bill Hybels in 1996, it opened up a whole new world of ministry and mission for me. It expanded my vision of what church *could* be, but not at the expense of what I had always assumed church *should* be. I read these words of confirmation from Bill Hybels in his introduction:

> I can honestly say that building a big church was never the conscious desire of my heart. I never set out to see how innovative I could be with drama or music, or how many cultural codes I could crack. Those were simply a few means to an incredibly valuable end. What motivated me twenty years ago, and what motivates me today, is the priceless goal of seeing redeemed people become the church.[1]

---

[1] Lynne Hybels and Bill Hybels, *Rediscovering Church: The Story and Vision of Willow Creek Community Church* (Grand Rapids, MI: Zondervan, 1995), 13–14.

The message of the cross was not absent from the Hybelses' vision for a new kind of church. "We need to be reckless purveyors of saving grace," they said. "In the end, it's only this love of Christ that can change [us]."[2]

This book, along with Rick Warren's *The Purpose Driven Church*[3] and the blueprint for a seeker-targeted model of ministry they presented, scratched a big itch for me and for many others. And it wasn't because they planned to discard the gospel.

But the problem, as many of us see it now, is that this message of the cross appears to have gotten lost despite our best intentions, contrary to plan, obscured in the well-meaning zeal to remove the unnecessary barriers. In one church I was a part of, they literally removed a cross from the sanctuary wall because it seemed too churchy. (It actually wasn't so much churchy as cheesy, made of Plexiglas and wire.) There's not really anything wrong with having or not having a cross on your church walls, but for many of us, in retrospect this removal became symbolic of what seemed to be taking place message-wise.

Now, many attractional churches still preach that Jesus died for our sins, of course. But too often this message of Christ's death has become assumed, the thing you build up to rather than focus on. Or, in too many other cases, this message is treated as the "add-on" to other messages, the proposition presented at the end of a message that is more about our personal success than Christ's personal victory.

A cognitive dissonance can result for those who hear a message all about what they should do to be more successful or victorious or happy or what-have-you, only to then hear the proposition that Jesus died for our sins. To hear a lengthy appeal to our abilities, culminating in an appeal to our utter inability, can cause spiritual whiplash.

But the appeal is easy to see. Attractional is certainly attractive.

---

[2] Ibid., 164.
[3] Rick Warren, *The Purpose Driven Church* (Grand Rapids, MI: Zondervan, 1995).

These kinds of messages, over time, communicate to seeker and believer alike that Christianity is about themselves, making the faith more about self-improvement or life enhancement—which are things we all want deep down. But are they the real message of Jesus?

The dominant message in so much attractional preaching is that Jesus has come to make life easier or better for us, that his teachings can help us in pursuit of our aspirations. So the attractional church sometimes struggles to talk about sin. Not always, of course, but sometimes. Sin is recast as problems, baggage, "issues," brokenness, all real and true things but none quite getting at what sin really is—a cancer deep inside all of us that is a hideous offense against the holiness of God.

This, of course, is not speaking the attractional church's language at all! I know, because I've been there. Right now, if you are committed to the attractional church model, you may be taking issue with my claims, saying the gospel is the ever-present reason behind everything you do and that it's exactly "Christian-ese" like this talk about cancerous sins and offending the holiness of God that turns lost people off. And you may think that churches that focus on that kind of stuff will never have the kind of impact churches can have when they focus on more positive things.

Because the proof is in the pudding, right? If the attractional message didn't work, the attractional churches would not be filled with people (and getting bigger by the week).

But maybe numbers don't tell the whole story.

What If Perception Is Not Reality?

When it comes to influence, could it be that Christians have a perception problem? Consider the issue of "celebrity Christianity." Idolization of celebrities is, of course, a problem in any culture. Within evangelicalism, however, we have our own common celebrities—Billy Graham, Rick Warren, Joel Osteen, et al. And then each tribe within evangelicalism has its own set of celebrities—John Piper and Matt Chandler and Tim Keller in one, Perry Noble and Steven Furtick and Craig Groeschel in another, T. D. Jakes and Benny Hinn and Paul Crouch in yet another. The emergents and progressives, for all their rhetorical rejection of consumerism and hierarchicalism, have their own celebs too.

We look at our guys who have "platforms" and project their influence into the world wider than it actually is. I've walked with Matt Chandler around a conference venue and experienced how intense it is to be met at every step with folks who want to say hi or thanks or tell him their story or get him to sign their Bible(!)—to each of which interruptions he responds with great patience and grace. And then I remember talking with him later and saying something like, "You probably can't even go out to eat in Dallas without being recognized."

"Nah," Matt said. "You have to really be somebody to get recognized in Dallas. If I was T. D. Jakes, maybe . . ."

It put things in clearer perspective for me that this guy that many of us consider a huge celebrity in the Christian world wouldn't even get noticed in his own town. His statement put Christian celebrity culture in its rightful place.

Perception, however, has become reality. We can see this as we hear statements like the one I read this morning on Facebook from a young woman who used to attend my young adult ministry in Vermont. She was objecting to the biblical pattern for church governance and church discipline because it simply has become irrelevant, given "all these massive churches." In her mind, evangelical churches have become so huge, they can no longer be expected to accommodate the outdated structures laid out in the Bible (notwithstanding Acts 2:41 telling us that three thousand souls joined the church in one day, I guess). Now, this young woman once lived in Vermont, so she knows that massive churches aren't the norm everywhere. But she now lives in the South, where massive churches very much are part of the regular evangelical perception. Perception has become reality.

But the actual reality is quite different from many of our perceptions.

First of all, I think evangelicals have an overinflated sense of the numbers, which in turn distorts the big picture. The presumption is that big, attractional churches are the norm, mainly because it is the big, attractional churches that get most of our media coverage. It is the big, attractional church pastors who get book deals and speaking engagements. When celebrities go to church, they typically land at big, attractional churches. When the media does news reports about churches, they tend to focus on the big, attractional churches. The bigger platforms take up the biggest real estate in our evangelical vision. That's not necessarily either good or bad. It just is.

But it can distort our perception of the evangelical landscape. According to Duke University's 2010 National Congregations Study, the median church size in the United States is 75 regular participants.[4] And when they calculated the approximate distribution of churches in the nation based on size—including Protestant and other Christian churches but excluding Catholic and Orthodox churches—they learned that churches with 1,000 or more regular participants constituted only 2.5 percent of all churches. Churches running 500–999 regular attenders account for only 4 percent of all churches. Instead, what we might call "small churches" today, the ones whose pastors do not get book deals or speaking invites, account for the vast majority of churches in the country—those with 100–499 people make up 35 percent of all churches, and those with 7–99 make up 59 percent.

The perception that most churches are big, or even that the most successful churches (when measuring things like reproduction, for instance) are big churches is simply that—perception.

---

[4] "Fast Facts about American Religion," Hartford Institute for Religion Research, http://hirr.hartsem.edu /research/fastfacts/fast_facts.html#sizecong.

But while they still remain the minority in the evangelical church landscape, the number of big churches is increasing, and the big churches are getting bigger. Statistics bear this out as well:

[I]t is evident that the number of megachurches per million Americans is increasing at an ever faster rate. Not only are there more megachurches, but also there are more megachurches per million Americans now than previously, and they are growing more rapidly than the population.[5]

But what if the numbers don't represent the people we think they do?

What If We're Not Reaching Those Whom We Think We Are?

In 1995, Sally Morgenthaler published *Worship Evangelism*, in which she articulated and pioneered the blueprint for seeker/ attractional church worship. Morgenthaler became an in-demand speaker and writer, and the principles she defended so well became standard for many attractional churches, even ones who had never heard of Morgenthaler and her book. Her idea was simply that "God designed worship to witness . . ."[6]

This is absolutely true. Worship is witness. And, in fact, witness is worship. The theological point is sound: when believers are engaged in the worship of God, this worship communicates to a lost world who God is and what he has done. Morgenthaler goes on to explain that when believers demonstrate that the deepest longings of our hearts are satisfied by God, it bears compelling witness to those who are seeking the same kind of satisfaction.

This theological truth is played out practically by the idea that the worship service in particular—the regular gathering of believers to hear from God's Word and exalt him in worship—ought to be

---

[5] Scott Thumma and Dave Travis, *Beyond Megachurch Myths* (Hoboken, NJ: John Wiley, 2007), 7.
[6] Sally Morgenthaler, *Worship Evangelism* (Grand Rapids, MI: Zondervan, 1999), 79.

conducted with the aim of bearing witness. So Morgenthaler cites multiple practitioners of "worship evangelism," including mega-church pastors who design multiple services with different styles and "feels" (their word, not mine) to reach a variety of kinds of seekers. It is not uncommon now for large churches not just to offer multiple services or campuses to accommodate more people but to offer multiple genres or "experiences" in these venues to accommodate more tastes and preferences.

If the purpose of worship is evangelism, this makes sense. So to advertise our worship experiences we add adjectives that communicate the intended effect. We call our worship "dynamic" or "exciting" or "engaging." The unintended message is that worship is not for God but really for the worshiper. Which raises the question, Who are we worshiping?

Unfortunately, the net effect of worship evangelism has not been pleasing, and now Sally Morgenthaler has essentially disavowed her own claims. In conducting research into the fruit of the movement she was instrumental in building, she has concluded that the seeker church hasn't exactly accomplished what it aimed to accomplish. She has the data to prove it.

Morgenthaler writes of this great unraveling:

> The realization hit me in the gut. Between 1995 and 2000 I'd traveled to a host of worship-driven churches, some that openly advertised that they were "a church for the unchurched." On the good occasions, the worship experience was transporting. (I dug a little deeper when that happened. Invariably, I found another value at work behind the worship production: a strong, consistent presence in the community.) Too many times, I came away with an unnamed, uneasy feeling. Something was not quite right. The worship felt disconnected from real life. Then there were the services when the pathology my friend talked about came right over the platform and hit me in the face. It was unabashed self-absorption, a worship culture that screamed, "It's all about us" so loudly

that I wondered how any visitor could stand to endure the rest of the hour.[7]

I remember the morning this became clear to me in terms of my own church experience. I'd long suspected the worship experience at our church was aimed more at the congregation's sense of excitement and engagement than at God's worthiness and exaltation. Certainly there is nothing wrong with feeling good when celebrating God's character and work. But if the purpose of worship is to feel good, we stop worshiping God. This realization had been dawning on me for a while, and it was solidified into sobering conviction when one of our worship leaders turned to her partner and announced in the intro to a particularly rousing song, "It's the Bev and Shirley Show!"[8]

That is an extreme example, but in an odd sense the admission, unwitting though it was, is refreshing. Another time we were led to sing along with a song off the indie rock station, "With My Own Two Hands," by Ben Harper. The lyrics read in part, "I change the world with my own two hands. Make it a better place with my own two hands. Make it a kinder place with my own two hands."

I know the idea behind that song choice, and can sympathize with it. But in this case it would seem that the outworking of the intention to make worship a relevant witness constituted worship of ourselves.

Morgenthaler's research went further than simply questioning the focus of the worship; she came to question the results of such "worship evangelism":

In 2001 a worship-driven congregation in my area finally did a survey as to who they were really reaching, and they were shocked. They'd thought their congregation was at least 50

---

[7] Sally Morgenthaler, "Worship as Evangelism," *Rev!* magazine (May–June 2007), 49, http://nancybeach .typepad.com/nancy_beach/files/morgenthaler_article.pdf.
[8] Names have been changed.

percent unchurched. The real number was 3 percent. By 2002 a few pastors of praise and worship churches began admitting to me that they weren't making much of a dent in the surrounding non-Christian population, even though their services were packed and they were known for the best worship production in town. Several asked me to help them crack the unchurched code. One wanted to invest in an expensive VJ machine and target twentysomethings. The others thought a multisensory, ancient-future, or emergent twist might help. However, when I visited their congregations, it wasn't hard to see that the biggest barrier to reaching the unchurched had little to do with worship technique or style.[9]

But if, as we've already established, the number of megachurches is increasing and the size of these megachurches is also increasing, what can account for this growth aside from evangelism? Morgenthaler's research calculates thusly:

Between 1994 and 2004, church attendance in congregations between 1,000 and 2,000 grew 10.3 percent. Congregations over 2,000 grew 21.5 percent. According to a Hartford Seminary study titled "Megachurches Today 2005," there are 1,210 Protestant churches in the United States with weekly attendance over 2,000, nearly double the number that existed in 2000.

Yet, according to The Barna Group, the number of adults who did not attend church nearly doubled in the same time period. In a parallel trend, pollsters were charting the lowest ratings for religion in 60 years. With both numbers and attitudes of the unchurched going in the opposite direction, where was all the growth in these big-and-getting-bigger churches coming from?

Location just might be a clue. Nearly 72 percent of churches with average weekly attendance of at least 2,000 people are found in a swath from Georgia and Florida across Texas to

[9] Morgenthaler, "Worship as Evangelism," 49–50, http://nancybeach.typepad.com/nancy_beach/files/morgenthaler_article.pdf.

California . . . roughly the Bible Belt and the most churchgoing sectors of the Sun Belt. It's hard not to see the correlation.[10]

Morgenthaler's data is consistent with other recent studies as well. Nearly every major statistical survey into American church life is showing that the nation is becoming less and less churched, even as megachurches become bigger and more common.

It turns out that while megachurches are flourishing, America has suffered an actual *net loss* of churchgoers since the rise of the seeker/attractional movement. This means that the seeker/attractional movement has not succeeded. It meant to get lost persons in the doors and make them "fully devoted followers of Christ," and in the fifteen years or so of their model's predominance, American churches are actually less full across the board.

So who's filling all these churches? Every week, some of the attractional leaders post growing numbers of baptisms and "decisions." What can we conclude?

As the research shows, by and large the people filling these church buildings week in and week out turn out to be other Christians. Often they are de-churched Christians or disaffected Christians or disillusioned Christians, but the idea that the attractional church is having its doors beaten down by lost people is a myth.

What generally happens is that an aspiring megachurch develops an attractional mind-set, and their efforts produce great fruit in attracting Christians from other churches with less prodigious offerings, or Christians who have been out of church for a while. These folks need church too, of course. But the kind of growth the attractional church experiences the most of is in reality the kind of growth they often claim they don't want, the kind we might call "transfer growth."

What we see happening most often is that a Christian bored or unsatisfied with the goods and services at his church goes to

---

[10] Ibid., 51.

the more attractive church with the more rockin' worship, more dynamic preacher, fancier facility, better coffee, bigger kids' or students' ministry, etc., but five to six years later (and in many cases, even less), they become dissatisfied with *that* experience and are ready to go find another.

It seems in fact that the very paradigm of the attractional church creates this instability. As a church seeks to speak into a particular demographic or life stage, channeling significant resources into certain key areas of a church, it ends up attracting people whose life stage or circumstances most resonate with those offerings. But when they stop resonating, they stop going. So the retention rate for the attractional megachurch is not very promising.

A young family may begin at a particular church because it has a high-impact children's ministry and a worship style that fits with young Mom and Dad's tastes. But then the kids get older, and so do Mom and Dad. It seems important, then, to find the church with the best student ministry. Then, when the kids are gone, and it's just Mom and Dad at home, finding themselves suddenly in middle age, the worship style they found so resonant at the younger churches seems too young, and they long for perhaps more substantial preaching or for a church more focused on men's ministry or social justice issues.

Do you see what has happened? The family has not been won to a church. They've been won to a menu of attractive goods and services.

So just counting the numbers does not tell us the whole story. It doesn't ensure for us that we are doing the things the Bible actually calls the church to do. We may argue that we are called to be fishers of men and that the increasing size of our churches proves we are doing just that, but if we go beneath the counting of heads, inside the heads themselves, the emerging data is showing that:

- most of the people coming to the attractional church are already professing believers,

- most of the believers coming to the attractional church remain in one church for a relatively short period of their lives, and
- most of the people in the attractional church are not effectively discipled toward spiritual growth beyond the seeker or consumeristic stage of life.

You may argue these points, and you are of course welcome to do so. For many, the numeric size and growth of a church are justification enough for whatever it is doing. And while there is nothing inherently wrong with bigness—anyone who says they don't want their church to grow this way is either lying or suffering from a martyr complex—size does not tell us all we ought to know. Indeed, size does not even seem to be the primary measurement the Bible uses to help us measure the faithfulness of our churches.

What if the way we measure obscures the reality that our system is broken? What if we're measuring the wrong things?

What If Bigger Isn't Necessarily Better?

The paragon of the attractional church model itself, Willow Creek, published its REVEAL survey a few years ago, demonstrating the sobering reality that much of what they thought they were doing to cultivate disciples hadn't worked:

> The study shows that while Willow has been successfully meeting the spiritual needs of those who describe themselves as "exploring Christianity" or "growing in Christ," it has been less successful at doing so with those who self-report as being "close to Christ" or "Christ-centered." In fact, one-fourth of the last two groups say that they are either "stalled" in their spiritual growth and/or "dissatisfied" with the church.[11]

Basically what happened was this: Willow Creek discovered that after putting a lot of resources, expertise, volunteers, and years into

---

[11] "What *Reveal* Reveals," *Christianity Today* 52/3 (March 2008): 27, http://www.christianitytoday.com/ct /2008/march/11.27.html.

the development of fully devoted followers of Christ, the system didn't work. It was a brave admission, and Willow stood to lose a lot of credibility in the church world by making it. Their honesty was bold and staggering.

The results of the study, also conducted in other attractional churches around the country with similar results, were like a splash of cold water on the face of the attractional movement. The shock was hard. And you would have thought it would have had lasting implications. But it seems that, after the news cycle spun on, everyone just sort of shrugged and went back to business as usual.

My fear is that there is too much at stake here for many churches. As Willow did, they have put so much time and energy and money into their system. Way too much to consider for longer than a minute that it might have been an inefficient use of resources at best, a wasteful use at worst.

No one can doubt that the attractional church model has won souls to Christ. We should also agree that people have found Christ through the fundamentalist movement, through skeezy revival services under sweaty tents, by reading those creepy Chick tracts, in the middle of traditional services and charismatic services and from watching TBN and through people simply minding their own business walking down the street. God will use anything to bring people to him. But just because he is no snob, that doesn't mean "anything" is normative for our use. The ends don't justify the means.

In any event, only a dishonest critic would argue that no one gets saved through the attractional church. Perhaps more people find Christ at such churches today than in the so-called traditional church. Any church seriously looking to reach the lost will have a greater advantage in reaching the lost than the churches that don't. That's just math.

We can even acknowledge that the worship service as "evangelistic tool" is not an entirely invalid idea. Honest, authentic worship that exalts God and genuinely speaks from the human condition can be attractive and invitational, as real honesty can be.

But in seeking to define success the way the Bible does, we have to be brave and admit we aren't doing as well as we think we are. Even by the attractional church's own standard of measurement—effectively reaching the lost—the actual numbers, again, show that more disaffected Christians are being reached than the lost.

So Willow Creek sought to apply their metrics to the realities beneath the reality. They managed to assemble a very big church with a very big reach. But what if those numbers belied a failure of their fundamental reason for existence?

Well, they did. If all Willow wanted to do was build a huge church, mission accomplished. But if they wanted to disciple people into maturity in Christ . . .

One thing the REVEAL study proved is that one can have the appearance of success and yet not actually be succeeding. I think of the prophetic vision of the valley of dry bones in Ezekiel 37. The Lord deposits Ezekiel into this dry landscape, holding out the prospect of a time of refreshing, of revival. The bones must live! But there comes an interesting development in the unfolding vision, on the way from dead bones to a great living army. We see it in Ezekiel 37:7–8:

> So I prophesied as I was commanded. And as I prophesied, there was a sound, and behold, a rattling, and the bones came together, bone to its bone. And I looked, and behold, there were sinews on them, and flesh had come upon them, and skin had covered them. But there was no breath in them.

He's gathered a crowd! Sometimes the gospel will do that. Sometimes we can do that without the gospel. It's not too difficult to attract a crowd, if you know what you're doing. But crowds can be deceiving.

Ezekiel 37:7–8 shows us that something can *look* alive but not actually be alive. It's possible for what's been assembled to look successful, to look active, and yet not be filled with the Spirit of God.

Is it possible this is what we've crafted with many of our ecclesiastic enterprises? Have we only set loose an army of shiny, platitude-dispensing golems? Spiritual skeletons clacking about in the religious busywork of Christian relevance but devoid of real meat on the bones?

To be fair, this reality is also prevalent in churches that pride themselves on having "sound doctrine," where human ingenuity and personality and tradition reign just as unself-consciously as in more contemporary churches.

It is a customary mantra of ministry that healthy things grow. And yet sometimes healthy things shrink. This is certainly true of our bodies, when we're eating right and exercising. I mean, the formula doesn't always work in every circumstance. "Healthy things grow" sounds right. But cancer grows too.

Jesus warned against the leaven of the Pharisees and the leaven of Herod precisely for this reason: we may mistake the rising of something for the health or success of the thing. So it's possible to look big, to look successful, and to not actually be big or successful in the ways that matter.

This is not a strike against having a megachurch. It's only a strike against the idolatry of the megachurch. It's a strike against a church of any size that is trusting in growth, whether it's actually experiencing it or not.

I pastor a church in Vermont, not the smallest state in the nation (though close to it), but nevertheless the least-churched state in the nation. Vermont has the highest percentage of those who claim "None" on religious affiliation surveys. There is really no such thing as a megachurch here. Our biggest church is smaller than the smallest megachurch elsewhere. So as the Christians in our state begin to contemplate the future of mission and ministry here, it becomes important that in our zeal for "more" we don't end up measuring the wrong things.

When I arrived at our church in the little rural town of Middletown Springs, our average weekly worship attendance was about 40–50. In the five years since, we have more than doubled. We rarely count our attendance—not for any principled reason, really, just because no one thinks to do it— but the last time we did, we counted 110, not including the growing number of children. That's not a big church by our cultural standards, although we are well within the majority for church size across the nation, but we are "big" for our town (about 600 at last count) and, though we are not the biggest church in our county, 110 is still nothing to sneeze at for our area.

Probably to you, 110 seems pretty pathetic, and you wonder why you're even still reading this. I'd only suggest that running 18 percent of our town's population in worship and more than doubling in five years is pretty significant. At least, we like to think so. And yet, I have to constantly remind myself that this is not "the win." As great as it is to grow like this—and to keep growing like this!—we have to remind each other that it's possible to increase in numbers and at the same time decrease in health. Sometimes unhealthy things grow.

Sometimes healthy things grow, but the growth continues on in a momentum of its own and ends up obscuring areas of concern or deeper need that are easy to ignore because of the easy justification and visibility of the growth.

Is it possible that bigger isn't necessarily better?

It would seem, actually, that for some churches, *bigger* inadvertently becomes the point, and indicators of real spiritual growth and impulses of real missionary growth become subsumed in the energy channeled toward size. Neil Cole writes,

> There are millions of people in smaller congregations across the country who live with a feeling that they are failures because their church isn't as big as the megaplex congregation down the street. This is sad and should not be the case.

> A global survey conducted by Christian Schwartz found that smaller churches consistently scored higher than large

churches in seven out of eight qualitative characteristics of a healthy church. A more recent study of churches in America, conducted by Ed Stetzer and LifeWay Ministries, revealed that churches of two hundred or less are four times more likely to plant a daughter church than churches of one thousand or more. The research seems to even indicate that the pattern continues—the smaller the size of the church the more fertile they are in planting churches.

It pains me that so many churches and leaders suffer from an inferiority complex when in fact they could very well be more healthy and fruitful than the big-box church down the street.

I am not suggesting that the mega church is something we need to end, I am simply saying that we need other kinds of churches to truly transform our world. I also do not want people in huge churches to think that, just because they have more people and more money, they are more blessed by God. The stats tell us that ten smaller churches of 100 people will accomplish much more than one church of 1000.

Christian Schwarz says:

"The growth rate of churches decreased with increasing size. This fact in and of itself came as no great surprise, because in large churches the percentages represent many more people. But when we converted the percentages into raw numbers, we were dumbfounded. Churches in the smallest size category (under 100 in attendance) had won an average of 32 new people over the past five years; churches with 100–200 in worship also won 32; churches between 200–300 average 39 new individuals; churches between 300–400 won 25. So a 'small' church wins just as many people for Christ as a 'large' one, and what's more, two churches with 200 in worship on Sunday will win twice as many new people as one church with 400 in attendance."

Schwarz found that the average growth rate in smaller churches was 13% (over five years), whereas in larger churches it was a mere 3%. A small church in the NCD sample with an average attendance of fifty-one typically converted thirty-two persons in five years; megachurches in the NCD sample averaged 2,856 in attendance but converted only 112 new persons in five years. The same number of persons participating in fifty-six small churches averaging fifty-one in attendance would have produced 1,792 converts in five years.

I know such extrapolations in some ways mean little. I also know that conversions is not the whole picture. My point is that we need to stop seeing smaller churches as less successful. The trend currently is seeing the closing down of smaller churches as larger ones increase in size and number and I think this could be an alarming trend given the actual facts when we measure true influence.[12]

But again, the problem is not really one of size but of an unhealthy obsession with size, with a pitting of bigger against smaller, and with the failure of growing churches to compensate for their numeric growth with scalable efforts to maintain pastoral care, community, and discipleship. And what Cole and Schwarz are noting is the apparent statistical trend of bigger churches away from outward mission. Perhaps smaller churches are more missionally nimble. (In chapter 6 we'll talk about how a large or growing-large church might work toward missional nimbleness.) Can you consider that, perhaps, in the attractional model of church, it is not just difficult to effectively disciple people; it is also difficult to care for their souls?

What If People Aren't Being Pastored?

In too many attractional churches, committed Christians are put to work largely in service of the weekend worship experience, which is seen as the distinguishing mark of maturity, and single-minded

---

[12] Neil Cole, "Is Bigger Really Better? The Statistics Say 'No'!," ChurchPlanting.com, http://www.church planting.com/is-bigger-really-better-the-statistics-actually-say-no/#axzz2xMgsxk5q. "NCD" refers to the Natural Church Development organization, a network aimed at helping churches grow and minister according to biblical principles.

devotion to this end is expected, if not encouraged. In the beginning of such ministry, enthusiasm is high. But when the lion's share of one's discipleship is occupied with weekly efforts toward the worship service, it is not too long before the volunteers begin to feel interchangeable, like cogs in a wheel. They may begin to feel like simply a warm body. It could be anyone else moving chairs around, setting up lights, running the sound board, handing out nametags, checking in children for nursery, etc. All of those are worthy tasks, not too small to give glory to God. But if they are the sum total of one's connection to the church, they do not provide the nourishment that growing Christians need, to follow Christ in all areas of life.

Are we careful, also, when these worn-out volunteers speak up? If they ever so much as suggest something isn't right, they are sometimes accused of being immature. I have heard of such people being told to go "self-feed" (more on this in chapter 7). They are chastised for their request for care, told rather bluntly that church actually isn't for *them* but rather is for the lost people we are trying to reach. This is doubly hurtful when the volunteers are believers who were seekers or baby Christians when they first entered the church. Now they feel like the place that won them no longer needs them; they feel like they've outgrown the church. This can be an emotionally painful experience.

In Christine Wicker's *The Fall of the Evangelical Nation*, the author surveys attractional church burnout, which I've witnessed numerous times personally. Wicker writes,

> A large reason megachurches grow is because of where they usually locate—in burgeoning suburbs. Young families, attracted to the suburbs' less-expensive housing, want religion for their children. They're energetic, and they have rising incomes. Megachurches have enormous overhead and a huge need for volunteers. Burned-out megachurch staff members sometimes complain that they spend more time "feeding the beast" than

feeding the flock. Feeding the beast requires a constant hunt for "good" families. To the dismay of the more idealistic, good families don't mean those who need God the most but those who are committed, able, energetic, and prosperous. . . .

[Megachurches are] top heavy on services for members, which means they must have huge budgets to keep the pace. Their building programs, their missions, their children's programs, their worship services—all have to be top-rate, which requires top-rate staff and plenty of volunteers. At Willow Creek the children's programming alone requires a thousand volunteers a week. As quickly as megachurches burn out one family, they need to replace it. Add to their troubles the fact that their growth has been supported by location. They started in rapidly growing, young communities. As young families are priced out of communities served by megachurches, they'll move farther out, and the megachurches, pinned down by big-box facilities, won't be able to follow.[13]

This is not necessarily a megachurch problem. But it seems to be an intrinsic deficiency of the attractional model, whether it is carried out in a big, medium, or small church. The tendency is to treat members not as sheep who need to be fed but as oxen pulling the load.

Of course, church members should be expected to serve the church in a variety of ways. No one could biblically argue that growing in Christian maturity means not contributing to the life of a church body. But in the attractional model, all too often members are not contributing to the life of their church body but to the church's programming, to the—dare we say it?—*show*.

What If the System's Broken?

This is a big question to ask, perhaps an offensive one. But I'm daring you to ask it. Rather than reflexively and defensively assuming

---

[13] Christine Wicker, *The Fall of the Evangelical Nation* (New York: HarperOne, 2008), 105ff.

all is well, shouldn't we all—no matter how we do church—ask if what we're doing in and through our churches is actually what God would have us do? Shouldn't we measure our models against the means and methods found in the Scriptures?

I want to suggest that it's possible to get big, exciting, and successful while actually failing substantially at what God would have us do with his church. It's possible to mistake the appearance of success for faithfulness and fruitfulness.

Everything inside of you may be crying out that there's no way this is happening. God has called you to reach the lost, and it would seem that any means useful to that end would be an appropriate means to use. But I want you to consider that when it comes to proclaiming the gospel to the lost and feeding the sheep, we have to give great care to the means. And in fact, how we do church will have a direct impact on the quality of the results we get.

3

What Works?

The Bible is frustratingly vague on "how to do church." It would be so much simpler if it laid out a detailed and comprehensive blueprint for governance, programming, style, and the like. Of course, some do think the Bible's words on these matters are quite clear and quite simple, and that's why you and I don't invite these people over for coffee very often!

Most of us, instead, see the Bible's clarity on essential doctrines of theology and requisite characteristics for a church, but see in the early church's methodology a picture that tends to be more *des*criptive than *pre*scriptive. For instance, we (mostly) all see that the church ought to commemorate Christ's death and its meaning through the sacrament of Communion, or the Lord's Supper. Evangelicals can differ on the theology of the Eucharist, of course, but we also tend to maintain differences of opinion on how often we ought to take it, whether we should use real wine or grape juice, whether the bread should be leavened or unleavened, whether we should pass it out to the congregation or have the congregation come forward to receive it from a leader or by themselves at a sort of "self-serve" table, etc.

Again, some think the Bible is pretty clear on all these matters. I do not. And you probably don't either. And how to do Communion is just the tip of the methodological iceberg. What does the Bible say about church membership? If you agree that it teaches membership, what does it say about the membership process? What about governance? We see elders and deacons covered in the Bible, but should our churches be elder-led and member-governed, or elder-governed and staff-led, or some other variation? We don't rightly know, although we all make educated decisions with the biblical evidence before us, trusting God to help us be faithful stewards of all he's given us to know and do.

The bottom line is that the historical church has always agreed on the doctrinal bounds of orthodoxy, the theological claims that make Christianity *Christianity*—the Trinity, the deity of Christ, the incarnation, salvation by faith in Christ, etc.—but we have tended to vary on how we embody this theology in our church communities. One logical assumption many make, then, is that church methodology is fairly malleable. As long as we believe the right things, we are free to do pretty much whatever we want.

The church has always needed to contextualize the gospel for its time and culture. An evangelical church in the Bahamas may look different from an evangelical church in rural Kentucky, and that evangelical church in rural Kentucky may look different from an evangelical church in urban Kentucky, or urban Ireland. And yet, as we seek to do the good work of missionary contextualization, we have to make sure that we have not crossed lines into cultural accommodation, that we haven't inadvertently adopted some of the values and appetites of our cultural contexts that stand in opposition to the Bible.

In this way of thinking, then, while we have great freedom in contextualization, we also face a great danger. That the Bible is somewhat vague about specific methodologies does not mean every methodology is fair game. Not every method is neutral. We have to go deeper and test our working assumptions. Beneath the exercise of liberty in methodology is always a functional ideology driving our decisions. A "functional ideology" is the belief (or set of beliefs) in a church that often goes unstated but nevertheless drives the methods and practices of the church.

Let's consider an example. As I suggested, I don't believe the Bible is abundantly clear on all the methodology for Communion. There is some very clear teaching about the Supper that is nonnegotiable: one should do it in remembrance of Christ, and one should not take the meal in an unworthy manner (without properly discerning his body), etc. But some would say you can't use unfermented grape juice because the Lord used wine. I don't think that is necessary, and in our church we use plain grape juice. Some would say you should use only unleavened bread (like matzo crackers) in keeping with the Passover meal restrictions and to symbolize Christ's body being free of sin. (In the Bible, leaven is often a symbol for sin.) But I don't think it is wrong to use leavened bread. As you can see, I would affirm some flexibility in the elements of Communion. And yet, when I hear of some folks—usually in youth groups—celebrating "Communion" with Doritos and grape soda, I pause. Does our freedom extend that far? Is it being legalistic to suggest such a meal is inappropriate for the Lord's Supper? It may be a bridge too far to say such a meal is *sinful*, but surely we have some grounds for asking about underlying assumptions and functional ideologies at work in allowing such elements for the meal. I think it values a novelty and frivolity and "cleverness" that works against the picture of the meal in the Bible and what Paul says about it in his teaching.

In short, just because we think we *can* do something doesn't mean we *should*.

I think the evangelical church in the West is particularly susceptible to two primary ideologies that drive many of its ways of doing church today, and I think the attractional model is fundamentally built on these functional ideologies. These ideologies are *pragmatism* and *consumerism*.

If It Works, Work It?

Pragmatism is the way of thinking that says, "If it works, let's work it."

We need to be careful, however, not to confuse pragmatism with simply being practical. That is usually the kind of objection we get when we criticize pragmatism. Someone will remind us that people need to put their faith into practice. People need practical helps to live out their walk with Christ. I agree.

Pragmatism is not the same thing as being practical. The Bible is practical. All one has to do is read Proverbs to see how practical the Bible can be. But pragmatism is the kind of thinking that values a thing based entirely on its apparent practicality. Pragmatism judges the usefulness of a particular practice (or sometimes even a particular person) based on results. So, for instance, if you can get five thousand people through your church doors on Easter Sunday by giving away a car, then giving away a car is good. In the pragmatic way of thinking, the ends justify the means.

On the flip side of pragmatism's working whatever appears to work, the mentality also suggests that if something does not "work," then we *shouldn't* work it. That's certainly true at times. There are some areas where being pragmatic may be fitting. But in the spiritual economy of Christian ministry, I would suggest that pragmatism runs counter to the functional ideology of Scripture.

For one thing, it is predicated on a predetermined measure of success. It assumes a method's value is based on the demonstration of our desired results. So if we want to fill our church building, and we know giving away a car will do it, giving away a car becomes an okay thing to do. But what if simply filling our church building is not a neutral result? What if our motives for filling the building aren't good? What if we are valuing the numbers too much? What if we are channeling more thought toward the building being filled with people than we are toward people being filled with the Spirit?

There are so many variables involved that indict the pragmatic mind set, not the least of which is that we very often assume that the results we desire necessarily come from godly desires. Or that God has even asked us to achieve those particular results.

In 1 Corinthians 3:6 Paul says, "I planted, Apollos watered, but God gave the growth." He is assigning credit for results not to the methodological work of planting or watering but to God. Paul seems to be saying that results in ministry are contingent not upon our efforts but upon God's sovereign pleasure.

Or maybe it looks quite logical to you: Paul planted, Apollos watered, and in response, God gave the growth. But that is not what the verse says. It says "but"—"*but* God gave the growth." Not "and." Similarly, Proverbs 16:9 says, "The heart of man plans his way, but the LORD establishes his steps." We think we know where we want to go, but where we end up depends on God's will, not good ideas.

Those passages of Scripture should stifle our inclination to spiritual math—e.g., if we do certain things, God will respond in the way we want. Those verses are instead a reminder that we can do *our* work but we cannot do *God's*. Nor is his work contingent upon ours. It's just as possible that he wouldn't give growth. This appears to be the point of Jesus's parable of the sower and the seed:

> "A sower went out to sow his seed. And as he sowed, some fell along the path and was trampled underfoot, and the birds of the air devoured it. And some fell on the rock, and as it grew up, it withered away, because it had no moisture. And some fell among thorns, and the thorns grew up with it and choked it. And some fell into good soil and grew and yielded a hundred-fold." As he said these things, he called out, "He who has ears to hear, let him hear." (Luke 8:5–8)

The sower appears to be scattering the seed somewhat indiscriminately. He is not testing the soil. He doesn't know if the seed will take root in some places as opposed to others. He simply remains faithful to do his work. It is practical work, too. He is responsible for sharing the gospel. But whether the gospel finds purchase in particular hearts is entirely up to God. This is partly why Jesus says, "He who has ears to hear, let him hear." He's assuming that one cannot receive the word of truth without the spiritual ears to hear it.

The pragmatic spirit would incline the sower toward more strategy. He would test the soil; he would determine his target constituency; he would perhaps even genetically reengineer the seed.

In Isaiah 6, the Lord calls the prophet Isaiah to go preach his word. It's a very practical matter. But Isaiah's ministry, foreordained by God, would upset the applecart of the modern-day pragmatist. God tells Isaiah that people won't listen. That they will hate him. And in fact, the Lord promises that Isaiah will lose 90 percent of the people through his ministry. Now, tell me, is that the kind of ministry vision you would sign up for? If you were interviewing for a pastoral position in a church and promised them that you would shrink the church to 10 percent of its current numbers, do you think you would get the job? In the pragmatic way of thinking, faithful church ministry always results in growth. And it does! But not always in the ways we expect and desire.

Isaiah's mission cost his ministry 90 percent of the people. But the people who stayed got stronger in their faith, more healthy. And it was out of that "stump" (Isa. 6:13; 11:1) that the way of Christ emerged.

Pragmatism has a utilitarian ethos to it. It is by nature unspiritual. It has no room for discernment in it. So if Jesus lost the five thousand people who came to the all-you-can-eat buffet (John 6) because he started preaching himself as the true bread of life, the pragmatist would take him aside and explain that he was being reassigned from speaking to hospitality.

Mark Dever says, "The greatest threat to the gospel specific to today is the indirect challenge of pragmatism among evangelicals."[1]

---

[1] Mark Dever, "The Apparent Piety of Numerical Goals," Together 4 the Gospel online, http://t4g.org/2006/03/the-apparent-piety-of-numerical-goals/.

But pragmatism has essentially become the water that evangelical ministry swims in. Looking back on my early years of church
ministry, I see so much of the pragmatic influence on just about
everything we did. It was certainly in effect during my youth ministry days, when we trusted silly games and pizza parties to keep
kids entertained. It was certainly in the evangelistic strategy, as
when we taught our teens to seek to evangelize the "key kids" at
school—the quarterback, the cheerleader, the student body president. The hope was that if the key (meaning "cool") kids got saved,
it would make getting saved look cool. It was sort of a trickle-down
theory of mission.

What we would have been shocked to hear is that pragmatism
is anti-gospel. Pragmatism is anti-gospel because it treats evangelism as a kind of pyramid scheme aimed at people who have it all
together, not discerning that, in the Gospels, those most ripe for
the gospel were those at the bottom of the social caste system, the
undesirable, the non-influential. It also, in a way, inverts the Great
Commission. Effective evangelism is seen as the domain of the ex-
perts putting the church production together. The missional man-
date becomes less "go and tell" and more "come and see."

Pragmatism is legalistic, because it supposes that evangelism
can be turned into a formula for ready results. It functions in law
mode, because it assumes, "if we do *this*, then *that* will happen."
The pragmatist has forgotten that Christianity is supernatural, that
it is capital-S *Spiritual.*

Pragmatism reasons that God's ability to use anything means our
freedom to use everything. Pragmatism treats church methodology
like a vending machine. But, as Francis Schaeffer has said, "The
Christian life, true spirituality, can never have a mechanical solution.
The real solution is being cast up into moment-by-moment communion, personal communion, with God himself, and letting Christ's
truth flow through me through the agency of the Holy Spirit."[2]

---

[2] Francis Schaeffer, *True Spirituality* (Wheaton, IL: Tyndale, 1971), 88.

Of course, what Schaeffer is talking about is difficult to program. The intangible work of the Spirit is not something we can schedule in our Planning Center. However, what we do schedule in Planning Center can go with the grain of the Spirit's work or it can go against it. We ought to beware settling for the appearance of results or the reputation for success. We don't want to be one of those places indicted by the rumored Korean pastor who, after having visited the States and being asked what he thought of the American church, said, "It's amazing what the American church can do without the Holy Spirit."

The pragmatic approach of too many attractional churches aims for quantity in disciple making but suffers in quality. When you try to help the Holy Spirit, you quench him. So as the pragmatic spirit drives our methodology, the kind of discipleship culture that results is shallow and frequently artificial. Pragmatic discipleship makes pragmatic Christians. The way the church wins its people shapes its people. So the most effective way to turn your church into a collection of consumers and customers is to treat them like that's what they are.

This leads to the second major functional ideology underlying the attractional model: consumerism.

Give the Customer What He Wants?

It has been reported that Willow Creek pastor Bill Hybels once had a poster hanging near his office that read, "What is our business? Who is our customer? What does the customer consider value?"[3]

If you have any doubt that business principles drive the methodology of the attractional church model, there is at least some anecdotal proof of the connection very near and dear to the heart of one of the leading founders of the movement. In fact, when I swam in the attractional stream and cut my teeth on the attractional

---

[3] James B. Twitchell, *Shopping for God: How Christianity Went from In Your Heart to In Your Face* (New York: Simon & Schuster, 2007), 254.

resources, one of our favorite go-to manuals was *Inside the Mind of Unchurched Harry and Mary*, by Lee Strobel.[4] "Harry and Mary" were stand-ins for the seeker demographic the attractional church was most interested in. This book was essentially an evaluation of our target consumer, and the line between religious customer and discipled Christian was erased.

This kind of professionalization thinking carried through into what's called the "church growth movement." We see the business terminology used in countless church growth resources, like those from leadership guru Aubrey Malphurs, who echoes Hybels's poster by writing in his book on a new model for church methodology, "[T]he business world asks, What does the customer want? The answer involves the customer's needs."[5]

But when we meld this kind of business principle into the functional ministry of the church, we make at least one crucial mistake: we assume that the customer's interests are legitimate.

People in the world of business often say, "The customer is always right." It is a law they faithfully obey, in the interest of excellent customer service.

My dad has worked in the retail world for most of his adult life. After a short stint as a junior and senior high teacher and coach, he began his business career with the department store Montgomery Ward in the late-'70s and has worked for a variety of department store and media store chains ever since. I remember him coming home one day and telling an astounding tale of exceptionally frustrating customer service. Some guy had purchased a huge television. (This was in the day before flat screens.) He proceeded to strap it to the roof of his car, despite cautions from the store clerks against this precarious perch. Well, what you can imagine happened, happened. At some point in his journey home, this guy's TV came loose and fell off his car into the street and was destroyed.

---

[4] Lee Strobel, *Inside the Mind of Unchurched Harry and Mary* (Grand Rapids, MI: Zondervan, 1993).
[5] Aubrey Malphurs, *Advanced Strategic Planning: A New Model for Church and Ministry Leaders* (Grand Rapids, MI: Baker, 2005), 132.

So the customer did what any clear-thinking human being ashamed of his own foolishness would do. That's right, he went back to the store and asked for a replacement.

This probably would not happen today, but in the 1980s business world, the customer was *always* right, so the guy got a new TV. If you want to serve your customers, in order to turn them into lifelong customers, you give them what they want. The customer is always right. But in my dad's mind—in the world of logic and realism and fairness—the customer is sometimes pretty stupid.

Of course, not all customers are stupid. But in the biblical way of thinking, if we're going to call potential believers customers, we have to acknowledge that sometimes the customer isn't right. And, in fact, sometimes the customer doesn't know what they want, or they want things that aren't very good for them, or they want things that aren't bad but aren't best.

No human's desires are value-neutral. We can and should address some felt needs, but not all felt needs are created equal.

But in the attractional model, great care and concern is given to identifying target customers and giving them the experience they want. This is why we often hear things out of attractional church leaders like, "When it comes to the quality of production, our worship services should rival Disney or Broadway," or "We want to be the Ruth's Chris of churches, not the Golden Corral."

The functional ideology of consumerism highlights the "felt needs" of,

- *Freedom of choice.* Here is an implicit rejection of authority where the customer—here, a churchgoer—chooses a church based on his preferences or tastes. Self-denying worship of God is not in view, since worship of God is *assumed*. The real matter in selecting a church to attend has less to do with the object of worship (God) and more to do with which worship experience is most to the worshiper's liking. Still less is a church selected based on the need of the community for the customer's gifts and edifying presence. The community is seen primarily as the dispenser of gifts and edification to the customer, not as recipient of them *from* the customer.

* *Competition in providing an experience.* Because the church is seen not as a community to participate in so much as a satisfier of felt needs and a pleaser of personal preferences, the attractional church model necessarily gives rise to competition among churches, as places of worship inadvertently begin to compete for market share with other churches in their area. A churchgoer weighs the offerings of the various nearby churches, comparing all their elements to determine which provides the most pleasing experience, which provides the best return on his attendance investment. Some may choose a church because it has an obvious opening in an area of service, but most make their choice because the quality of preaching or music or the various services (children's ministry, youth ministry, men's and women's ministry, etc.) are better than the competition's. Some attractional churches implicitly play into the competition in experience when, for instance, they advertise with slogans like "A church you can wear blue jeans to!" or "Not your grandfather's church."

* *Customization of product.* The savviest (and most well-resourced) of attractional churches understand that in order to attract and keep the greatest number of customers, they must increase and diversify the number of their offered goods and services. The easiest way to do this in the beginning is to multiply the number of worship experiences, offering them at strategic times throughout the weekend. Many churches make this concession simply to keep up with attendance growth. But many attractional churches begin also tailoring their individual services for particular tastes. So you can attend the contemporary service at 8 a.m. or the traditional service at 10 a.m.; you can come to the emerging worship experience on Saturday nights or the coffee-shop type casual experience on Sunday nights. Or you can simply stay at home and "attend" a virtual campus on the Internet. The more the attractional church can customize its offerings to reach as many kinds of

customers as possible—in the mind driven by consumeristic ideology—the better.

Freedom of choice, competition in providing experience, and customization of product. When you put this recipe into church strategy, you end up not with churches but with religious resource centers.

In the end, as in the beginning, the attractional church operating on pragmatic and consumerist principles has forgotten who the church is really *for*. They've forgotten who the audience for worship really is. It is not primarily the customer, not even the genuinely unbelieving seeker. As important as it is to reach seekers as part of the church's primary mission to make disciples, the target audience of the "worship experience" is not any mortal in the congregation. The target audience is God himself.

D. A. Carson writes, "What ought to make worship delightful to us is not, in the first instance, its novelty or its aesthetic beauty, but its object: God himself is delightfully wonderful, and we learn to delight in him."[6] What he means is that the primary purpose of a worship experience is the exaltation of God, the delighting in him as worthy to receive all glory and honor and power and praise. This isn't to say that the worship service shouldn't be aesthetically beautiful. Excellence in our worship adorns the gospel of God. In that sense, the quality of our experience is ornamental, a decoration we put around our central focus: the triune God himself and his mighty, saving deeds in Christ. But we aren't to worship the ornament. Too often in our churches, not just the attractional ones, we tend to worship worship itself. We end up saying things like, "That service didn't feel very worshipful," or "It's hard for me to worship to that style of music." Such statements aren't always inappropriate, of course, depending on what is meant by them. But we have to be careful that we don't mean

---

[6] D. A. Carson, "Worship under the Word," in D. A. Carson, ed., *Worship by the Book* (Grand Rapids, MI: Zondervan, 2002), 30.

that we go to worship to receive a certain feeling or encounter a particular emotional or psychological experience. The purpose of the worship service is not what we get out of it but the God who has drawn us into it.

In his invaluable book *The Divine Commodity*, Skye Jethani reproduces a conversation between economist James Gilmore (author of *The Experience Economy*) and *Leadership Journal* staffers Marshall Shelley (MS), Eric Reed (ER), and Kevin Miller (KM) that gets to the problematic heart of the attractional church's drive toward "experience":

> *MS:* So how does all this "experience providing" apply to the church?
>
> *Gilmore:* It doesn't. When the church gets into the business of staging experiences, that quickly becomes idolatry.
>
> *MS:* I'm stunned. So you don't encourage churches to use your elements of marketable experiences to create attractive experiences for their attenders?
>
> *Gilmore:* No. The organized church should never try to stage a God experience.
>
> *KM:* When people come to church, don't they expect an experience of some kind? Consumers approach the worship service with the same mindset as they do a purchase.
>
> *Gilmore:* Increasingly you find people talking about the worship *experience* rather than the worship *service*. That reflects what's happening in the outside world. I'm dismayed to see churches abandon the means of grace that God ordains simply to conform to the patterns of the world.
>
> *KM:* So what happens in church? Are people getting a service, because they're helped to do something they couldn't do on their own, that is, get closer to God? Or are they getting an experience, the encounter with God through worship?

Gilmore: The word "getting" is, I think, the problem with contemporary Christianity. God is the audience of worship. What you get is, quite frankly, irrelevant as a starting point.

ER: But people, especially unchurched people, don't perceive it that way. They're expecting some return.

Gilmore: They come that way at first: "Give me, feed me, make me feel good." But they should be led to say, "Hey, this is not about *me*, God. Worship is to glorify *you*."

KM: But if my mission is to reach a consumerist culture—if I'm going to get a hearing for my message—then I'm going to have to provide something that the consumer considers of value.

Gilmore: That is the argument. But the only thing of value the church has to offer is the gospel. I believe that one result of the emerging Experience Economy will be a longing for *authenticity*. To the extent that the church stages worldly experiences, it will lose its effectiveness.[7]

I'll say more about the worship experience in chapter 5, but for now it will suffice to say that in the attractional model, the center of worship is too often the preferences of the children and too rarely the proclamations of the Father.

Theologically speaking, the functional ideologies in the attractional church of pragmatism and consumerism are disastrous, because they make the individual person the center of the religious universe. This doesn't even serve the stated end of "making fully devoted followers of Christ," as Willow's REVEAL revealed, because when we treat our churchgoers like customers, we'll always lose out when they realize a better deal might be had elsewhere. And in the meantime, while we've got them, we are catering to their individualistic, subjective tastes and preferences, not training them

---

[7] Skye Jethani, *The Divine Commodity: Discovering a Faith beyond Consumer Christianity* (Grand Rapids, MI: Zondervan, 2009), 72–73.

to be like Christ, who emptied himself and gave up his life for the filling and building up of the church.

Pragmatism and consumerism also taint a church's numeric growth, because even as the place fills up with people, it may actually become less distinctively *a church*.

What If the Attractional Church Isn't?

That is to say, what if it isn't a church? How do you know when a gathering of people interested in singing spiritual songs and learning about God becomes less a church and more a . . . well, perhaps a religious society? A charitable organization? A concert?

I know this is a tricky charge to make, because nearly all pastors and their congregations—attractional, traditional, missional, what-have-you—believe and teach that the church is not a building, but the people who fill it. "The people are the church" is not revolutionary thinking, and nearly every minister would wholeheartedly endorse the idea.

However, as we talk about functional ideology (not just verbalized ideology) in this instance, we have to ask whether the nuts-and-bolts working of the attractional model is such that, for whatever intellectual assent is made to the fact that the church, like soylent green, is "peeeeople," the emphasis and focus is inevitably on making the machine go. Many attractional churches exist primarily to put on the best weekend worship service possible, and the bulk of the Monday to Saturday work of the church leadership is poured into service planning with the aim of creating that worship experience. Many attractional churches include in their list of expressed values "Quality" or "Excellence," by which they mean that their worship gathering will be done with a production rivaling Hollywood's best, and that the facilities will be extremely consumer-friendly.

Neither of those things is necessarily bad. Until, that is, they take over the life of the church leadership and ministry—as the church pursues its goal to put on an effective weekend service and to supply a positive experience for anyone who enters the building. The gap between congregant and pastoral staff grows, because the staff is too busy keeping the machine running to interact personally with the congregation. Community life actually suffers because nearly all of the energy is being poured into the community gathering. This is how the attractional model *functionally* treats church as a place.

Truer to the biblical portrait, on the other hand, is the church as a community that certainly values the worship gathering (and even the quality of the experience therein), but not as the central hope of evangelism or life change. Rather, missional testimony to God's work is seen as primarily being carried out through a church's congregants living lives of fragrant witness among their respective tribes.

The weekend church gathering is never seen in the Scriptures as a place where individuals go to enjoy a particular experience, nor as the central place of evangelism. When those things are the focus, the worship service loses its biblical identity, which in turn degrades the church's own identity. If you treat the worship gathering as an experiential production, in other words, the church begins to see itself as concertgoers or, again, as customers rather than as the body of Christ.

The worship service, biblically, is a gathering of Christians to enjoy God in communion with him and each other. There are several elements to this—singing, praying, preaching, eating. We could add other elements, too. But the service is meant to reorient the body around its head—Jesus Christ—and to prepare us for the ongoing personal and communal witness of the church outside the gathering. When the attractional church instead makes the worship service primarily an event for non-Christians, which invariably includes many non-Christian elements (to lower defenses and create comfort), it eventually moves from contextualization for the sake

of the culture to compromise with the culture, and throughout the
Bible we see this kind of merging with the world and diverging
from the true center corrupting the very identity of the people of
God. The attractional church follows a trajectory away from what
makes the church the church.

This obviously encompasses more than just the approach to the
weekend service, but this crucial shift in how one views the gathering leads us to our next question:

What Is the Role of the Gathering for the Seeker?

Here we must talk about the difference between being seeker-
targeted and being seeker-*mindful*. The worship service must be
conducted with the unbeliever in mind, but it doesn't need to be
conducted with the unbeliever in focus. The worship service can
be a very compelling witness to unbelievers present in the room—
and every church will have unbelievers in the room every Sunday;
some are just less clear than others on the reality of their unbelief.

The attractional model is the natural child of the seeker church
movement. As I earlier affirmed, the impetus behind the movement
is good; it is evangelistically minded. It takes very seriously Jesus's
profession that he has come to seek and save that which is lost. The
problem lies mainly in determining what church *is* and what its
gathering is for. The attractional model is primarily seeker-targeted
in that it says churches should primarily be about accommodating
the lost ("seekers") and therefore the worship gathering should be
designed around their presence. Thus follows the attractional shib-
boleth "relevance," and all the bells and whistles aimed at making
church feel less "churchy" and more like what unbelievers might
enjoy outside the church.

But in the biblical picture of the earliest church, we don't get any
indication that the worship gathering is meant to be an event oriented around the unbeliever's presence. In 1 Corinthians 14, where
Paul repeatedly uses the word "outsider" to refer to non-Christians,

he urges the gathered church to speak intelligibly and sensibly because of their presence in the assembly, but he does not assume that believers must speak directly and centrally to the outsiders present. He wants the church to be mindful of the visiting unbeliever, so that they can understand what is taking place and hear the gospel in a clear, compelling way. But he does not want the church to be focused on the visiting unbeliever or to conduct the service as if it were *for* the unbeliever. In 1 Corinthians 14:23, Paul speaks in such a way as to say, "*If* . . . outsiders or unbelievers enter," indicating that these cherished souls, when present, are not the regular focus of the gathering but occasional guests.

When we say the church's worship service is not meant to speak directly to the unbeliever, we don't mean that addressing the unbeliever is forbidden. Paul's exhortation not to allow tongues without an interpretation is a key point there, because he assumes such concession is a way to be hospitable and welcoming to outsiders—to speak, as it were, directly to them. He even goes so far as to say tongues are signs to the unbeliever, not the believer (1 Cor. 14:22).

This doesn't mean you need to start incorporating speaking in tongues in your worship service! (You may not even believe that gift is still in operation.) It just means that, for all this caution about whom the worship service is for and who its audience is, we are not ignoring the unbelievers present. Author Trevin Wax has offered a helpful comparison between the approaches of two pastors—Tim Keller of Redeemer Presbyterian Church in Manhattan, New York, and Andy Stanley of North Point Community Church in Atlanta, Georgia—with regard to this issue. Wax writes that,

> These two pastors come from different contexts (Atlanta vs. New York) and different theological streams (Baptistic non-denominational vs. confessional Presbyterian). What's more, they approach ministry from different starting points, then employ different methods to achieve their purposes. Despite

all these differences, there is one thing Stanley and Keller agree on: preachers ought to be mindful of the unbelievers in their congregation.[8]

Stanley's approach to preaching generally seems more directed at the unbeliever or new believer, while Keller's assumes of his target audience a greater interest in or familiarity with the biblical text, but both take care to be "seeker mindful." In explaining his seeker-mindfulness, Stanley says, "As a general rule, say what you suspect unbelievers are thinking. When you do, it gives you credibility. And it gives them space."[9] Keller concurs, in a way, saying, "We must preach each passage with the particular objections of that people group firmly in mind," noting that he will often say things like this in his sermons: "If you are not a Christian or not sure what you believe, then you surely must think this is narrow-minded—but the text says this, which speaks to this very issue . . ."[10]

Neither Stanley's nor Keller's style of sermon delivery may match our own, and that's generally okay. But we can learn from them their way of making allowances for the unbelievers present in the worship service, of offering a helping hand, as it were. It's good also to have a time of welcome in your service in which you greet visitors—believers and unbelievers alike—and let them know where they might find more information about the church or the gospel. It's good to include prayer for the unbelievers in corporate or pastoral prayers, asking God to grant them salvation.

So I'm not saying you pretend, in your service, that unbelievers aren't there. I'm only saying that designing your service (music, sermon, and everything else) specifically for them is neither biblical nor wise. We should not *assume* the presence of the *believer*, or ask them to be spectators or tolerators of a "seeker service,"

---

[8] Trevin Wax, "How Andy Stanley and Tim Keller Preach with Non-Believers in Mind," Send Network blog (April 2, 2014), http://sendnetwork.com/2014/04/02/andy-stanley-tim-keller/.
[9] Andy Stanley, quoted in ibid.
[10] Tim Keller, quoted in ibid.

because the worship service is, biblically speaking, meant to be their gathering. What the Bible seems to express is that unbelievers in the service are best served not by having their tastes catered to but by witnessing the gathered church exalting God in the receiving of Christ-centered teaching, the singing of God-centered songs, and the observing of the sacraments.

What You Win Them With Is What You Win Them To

In the last five or ten years or so, there has been a lot of concern in the evangelical world about the reported rate at which young adults (18–20s) drop out of the church. Some have placed it near 70 percent, although many of those are forecasted to return to church later in their lives. For every theory as to why this is so, there is a corresponding remedy. The attractional church did not grow up with the departure of the emerging millennials in mind—rather, this new way of doing church seems to have begun with the Baby Boomers working out their own cultural boredom with the church—but its aims have dovetailed quite nicely with the struggle to retain young adults. It seems, actually, that the attractional church as it operates today is very much in the spirit of the youth ministry models in which many of these millennials grew up.

The youth group culture that raised me in the faith (in the late-'80s through the mid-'90s) was chock-full of peppy songs (with corresponding hand motions), ridiculous games (Chubby Bunny, anyone?), outrageous scare tactics, silly videos, copious pizza, and the like. The messages were practical but invitational and tacked on to whatever shenanigans were used to lure us there and keep us in the room. I'm exaggerating, of course, but this kind of experience has become a cliché in the church for a reason—many of us actually experienced it. About this stuff, Matt Chandler has quipped, "It's a wonder anyone got saved in the eighties." But some of us did, of course, and the model perpetuates, because those raised in this culture who become ministers themselves begin to teach and implement what we've always known, cultivating the next generation of attractional student ministry.

One theory about the young adult drop-out rate is that kids raised in attractional student ministry up through their formative years to high school graduation do not have much bedrock faith to live on when they leave for the more disciplined and more intellectually rigorous world of college. Or those raised in this culture find the church they are expected to assimilate to post–youth group not as compelling as the youth group. The church of the grown-up world seems less fun, less entertaining, and therefore somehow less "relevant" than the faith of their youth.

The attractional church has in some ways responded to this reality by simply seeking to extend adolescent ways of faith and contextualization into the worship service and general life of the church. This may be a philosophical reach, to be sure, but I fear that many evangelical church leaders have not adequately explored the relationship between the dominant youth ministry culture of yesteryear and the production-minded, casually relevant attractional church culture of today.

What we do in church shapes us. It doesn't just inform us or entertain us. It makes us who we are. The worship service, in other words, doesn't just cater to certain tastes; it *develops* certain tastes. We will eventually be conformed to the pattern of our behaviors. Most of us instinctively understand this. Habits come from character, but it works the other way too—character is shaped by habits.

Brothers and sisters, we need to remember this truth: what we win them with is what we win them to. If we attract a crowd by appealing to their preferences, they are going to expect that we will continue to do so, and they will in fact eventually feel cheated or betrayed when we try to switch gears on them. It is not in the best interest of the very unbelievers we're trying to reach to appeal to consumerist tastes in the interest of offering them the living water of Christ. They've been drawn by the promise of lesser satisfactions. And when we make such a big production out of these lesser satisfactions, we communicate that in actuality they are what really satisfies.

As the production values begin to dominate our worship, we relay that it is the production that we find really compelling, not so much Christ himself. When the invitation to trust Jesus comes, if it ever does, Jesus feels a little like an awkward guest at someone else's party.

What you win them with is what you win them to.

The Vision Statement to End All Vision Statements

When we stage a worship experience that hypes up experience, feelings, or achieving certain states of success or victory, we miss the very point of worship itself: God.

And God is bigger than our feelings, bigger than our success. The one true God in fact is still the God of love and grace who is mighty to save by his Son through his Spirit when we are feeling tired, sad, or unsuccessful, or when we're not feeling anything at all.

Maybe, just maybe, by setting our worship experience sights so high, we've actually not set them very high at all. Maybe, as in C. S. Lewis's classic illustration, our reaching for exciting experiences and ever-present excellence is really a contentment for making mud pies while the holiday at sea remains uninitiated.

At the end of Acts 2 we find the compelling vision of the early church in action, "doing church" in a way that has captivated the evangelical imagination for years, including in the days of the burgeoning seeker church. It's from Acts 2 that Bill Hybels set forth his vision for the Willow Creek model in *Rediscovering Church*. It's Acts 2 that I remember my traditional-church-transitioning-to-seeker-church quoting from. My "Third Wave" charismatic friends quoted it too. I think they, as we, understand somehow that the future of the church lies back in its past, back there at the beginning. What did the apostles do? What did the early church do? What can we learn from them? Let's take another look:

> And they devoted themselves to the apostles' teaching and the fellowship, to the breaking of bread and the prayers. And awe came upon every soul, and many wonders and signs were being done through the apostles. And all who believed were together and had all things in common. And they were selling their possessions and belongings and distributing the proceeds to all, as any had need. And day by day, attending the temple together and breaking bread in their homes, they received their food with glad and generous hearts, praising God and having favor with all the people. And the Lord added to their number day by day those who were being saved. (Acts 2:42–47)

This is the picture of the church we all aspire to. This is the common "wish-dream" (to use Dietrich Bonhoeffer's words). We all want this description, and we think we know just what prescription is needed to see it become true of our own church experiences.

The early believers centered on the Word of God and through it on the church itself (v. 42). The resulting communal witness was compelling and powerful (v. 47). They did not, as far as we can tell, design their gatherings around appealing to the unsaved. They did not select music from the culture to help contextualize their witness. And yet they were blessed with many converts.

What made them this way?

Perhaps the answer is in the part of Acts 2 ignored by most of our vision statements, which focus only on these last few verses. Acts 2 begins with the outpouring of the Holy Spirit at Pentecost and continues with Peter's convicting evangelism, proclaiming the saving supremacy of Jesus Christ.

Do you want to evoke feelings? Acts 2:37 says Peter's audience was "cut to the heart." This gives way directly to that beautiful picture of the church in Acts 2:42–47. So what is the takeaway here? It is that the church will be built, strengthened, and driven into mission by the work of the Holy Spirit in the gospel of Jesus Christ. The Bible's "functional ideology"—contrary to consumerism and pragmatism—is that "what works" is the Holy Spirit through the message of the gospel of Jesus.

And neither the Spirit nor the gospel needs help from our production values.

4

The Bible Is Not an
Instruction Manual

Basic Instructions Before Leaving Earth.

Ever heard the Bible explained that way? It's a handy mnemonic that certainly has some truth to it. But does it get at the heart of what the Bible really is?

While being trained in the ministry, I learned how to craft sermons from listening to a lot of messages from our youth ministry, and from asking some pastors to help me. The gist of the enterprise was this: I needed to come up with a spiritual topic or "felt need" to address, something practical that my audience would be interested in or otherwise just needed to know. After identifying the topic, I needed to draft three to four sermon points, and these needed to be points of application, things my audience could actually *do*. The emphasis was constantly on practical application, not merely on intellectual information. The sermon needed some handles.

When my practical steps were listed, I needed to find biblical support for them. Anything that could not be supported with Scripture had to be rewritten or abandoned altogether. Every sermon had to be, in the parlance of the times, "Bible-based." (It is not uncommon now even to see on the websites of some attractional churches that their messages are "Bible-based" or that they offer "truth based on the Bible.") So then began the work of digging through the concordance to find Bible verses that might match and support each point.

It was typically a good idea to find a verse that used wording similar to the message point, and if you found something close, you could always tweak the message point to match the language of the verse or, alternatively, look at the verse in other Bible versions to see if the wording in one of those versions better matched the wording of the message point. This work could sometimes take just as long as writing the original applicational outline because we didn't use much Bible software back then, and of course the Internet (which today offers Bible Gateway and YouVersion and plenty of other resources) was not commonly used either. In the end, it was common to see a sermon that contained references from multiple Bible versions—the result of searching for just the right wording.

It took me many years to unlearn this approach to preaching. But in the end I began to discover that the approach was very much upside down. I had learned to preach by making the Bible's words serve what I wanted to say rather than by making my words serve what the Bible says. To teach and preach in this way is implicitly to say that the Bible can't be trusted to set the agenda, and that my ideas are better than the Bible at driving change in my audience. One prominent preacher says as much, as we'll soon see.

I've also come to see the Bible in a different way. I've always believed it was God's Word, of course, and that this makes it living and active (Heb. 4:12) and perfectly capable of making us complete Christians (2 Tim. 3:16–17). But I had been treating it more as a reference book than as a story, and more as a manual of good advice than as an announcement of good news.

So what is the Bible? The way so many of us trained in the attractional church came to see it—as God's "how to" book—doesn't seem quite right when we carefully look at what its own pages say.

And I fear that the way we used the Bible actually accomplished the opposite of what we intended.

The Shrinking Message of the Enlarging Church

For those of us who have felt convicted about the upside-downness of all the applicational teaching we've done, it stings when influential preachers whom many of us deeply respect suggest, as Andy Stanley once did, that the alternative of expository preaching is lazy. In an interview conducted by our mutual friend Ed Stetzer, Stanley says,

> Guys that preach verse-by-verse through books of the Bible—that is just cheating. It's cheating because that would be easy, first of all. That isn't how you grow people. No one in the Scripture modeled that. There's not one example of that.[1]

I have learned quite a bit from Andy Stanley and have used some of his resources in my church. But I find these words very unhelpful. I also think he is wrong on his two major claims: (1) that preaching "verse by verse" directly from Bible passages isn't how people grow; and (2) that there's no example of that in the Bible itself—and we'll see why, later in this chapter. For now, however, let's consider another question: What has been the net effect of the last several decades of the applicational focus? What is the fruit of having treated the Bible like an instruction manual?

As suggested earlier, it's my contention that when the church is run as a provider of spiritual goods and services, and slowly stops asking, first, "What glorifies God?" and begins asking more and more, "What do our customers want?" what the customer wants becomes more central in the life of the church. The functional ideologies of pragmatism and consumerism erode our theology, which becomes more flexible and less faithful.

---

[1] Ed Stetzer, "Andy Stanley on Communication (Part 2)," The Exchange blog (March 5, 2009), http://www.christianitytoday.com/edstetzer/2009/march/andy-stanley-on-communication-part-2.html.

The wider evangelical church is suffering terribly from theological bankruptcy. A recent Barna survey is particularly revealing. Their report reads in part,

> Overall, the current research revealed that only 9% of all American adults have a biblical worldview. Among the sixty subgroups of respondents that the survey explored was one defined by those who said they have made a personal commitment to Jesus Christ that is important in their life today and that they are certain that they will go to Heaven after they die only because they confessed their sins and accepted Christ as their savior. Labeled "born again Christians," the study discovered that they were twice as likely as the average adult to possess a biblical worldview. However, that meant that even among born again Christians, less than one out of every five (19%) had such an outlook on life.[2]

The Barna Group's research goes on to reveal that 79 percent of those identifying as "born again Christians" firmly believe the Bible is accurate in all its teachings—which is pretty good, I guess—but it also reveals that only 46 percent of these "born agains" believe in absolute moral truth, only 40 percent believe Satan is real, and only 47 percent strongly reject the idea that you can earn your way to heaven. Further, only 62 percent of the born again Christians surveyed strongly believe that Jesus was sinless.

This data is very sobering. It indicts evangelicals, yes, but surely it also indicts the information centers they are learning from. It demonstrates that over the last generation, not only has America become less Christian, but professing Christians have become less Christian. I think this is the direct result of evangelicalism's relentless prioritization of what seems useful over what is true. We have tended to favor the practical half-truth rather than the (allegedly) impractical whole truth.

---

[2] "Barna Survey Examines Changes in Worldview among Christians over the Past 13 Years," Barna Group (March 6, 2009), https://www.barna.org/barna-update/21-transformation/252-barna-survey-examines -changes-in-worldview-among-christians-over-the-past-13-years#.U0Ba417Wd_k.

Brothers and sisters, we ought to recover the roots of real Christianity before those who care are too few to do anything *useful* about it. Part of that recovery will involve identifying some of the factors that contribute to the problem. Some of these will be difficult to consider, but we ought to consider them anyway. Some of the problems we might explore are these:

1. Pastors are increasingly hired for their management skills or rhetorical ability over and above their biblical wisdom or their meeting of the biblical qualifications for eldership.

Our shepherds are increasingly hired for their dynamic speaking or catalytic leadership rather than their commitment to and exposition of the Scriptures, and for their laboring in the increase in attendance rather than the increase of gospel proclamation.

Now, of course, none of those contrasted qualities are mutually exclusive. Pastors can be both skillful managers and biblically wise; they can be both great speakers and great students of Scripture; and they can both attract crowds and proclaim the gospel. The problem is that, while they are not mutually exclusive, the latter qualities in each contrast have lost priority and consequently have lost favor. We have not prospered theologically or spiritually when we emphasize the professionalization of the pastorate.

2. The equating of "worship" with just one creative portion of the weekly worship service.

The dilution of the understanding of worship is a direct result of the dilution of theology in the church. The applicational, topical approach to Bible understanding has the consequence of making us think (and live) in segmented ways. The music leader takes the stage to say, "We're gonna start with a time of worship." Is the whole service not a time of worship? Isn't the sermon an act of worship?

Isn't all of life meant to be an act of worship?

One reason we have struggled to develop fully devoted followers of Jesus is that we incorrectly assign our terminology (equating worship with music only) and thereby train our people to think in truncated, reductionistic ways.

3. The prevalent eisegesis in Bible study classes and small groups.

"Eisegesis" basically means "reading *into* the Bible." It is the opposite of "exegesis," the process of examining the text and "drawing out" its true meaning. Many leaders today either don't have the spiritual gift of teaching or haven't received adequate training, and the unfortunate result is that most of our Bible studies are rife with phrases like, "What does this text mean to you?" as opposed to, "What does this text *mean?*" Application supplants interpretation in the work of Bible study, so it has become less important to see what the Bible means and more important to make sure the Bible is meaningful to us.

4. The vast gulf between the work of theology and the life of the church.

We have this notion that theology is something that takes place somewhere "out there" in the seminaries or libraries while we here at home are doing the real work of the Christian faith with our church programs. In many churches, theology is seen as purely academic, the lifeless intellectual work for the nerds in the church or, worse, the Pharisees.

5. Biblical illiteracy.

Our people don't know their Bible very well, and this is in large part the fault of a generation of wispy preaching and teaching (in the church and in the home). Connected to this factor is the church's accommodation and assimilation of the culture's rapid shifting from text-based knowledge to image-based knowledge. I'll say more about that in the next chapter, but when it comes to the text itself, I suspect that a lot of the superficial faith out there results from teaching that treats the Bible like *Bartlett's Familiar*

Quotations. Fortune-cookie preaching will make brittle, hollow, syrupy Christians.

6. *A theologically lazy and methodologically consumeristic/sensationalistic approach to the sacraments.*

The rise of the "scoreboard" approach to attendance reporting, some of the extreme examples of spontaneous baptism services, the neglect of the Lord's Supper or the abuse of it through fancifulness with the elements or lack of clear directives in presenting it—these are all the result of evangelicalism's theological bankruptcy. We don't think biblically about these matters, because we're thinking largely along the lines of "what works?" and consequently we might make a big splash with our productions but not produce much faith.

The source of all of these factors, if they may be reckoned accurate, is a fundamental misuse of the Bible by the leaders entrusted with preaching and teaching it. And the grand result of all of these factors is that as our churches get larger, our message keeps shrinking. We fill our buildings with scores and scores of people, but we've reduced the basic message to fit the size of an individualistic faith.

If the Bible is not essentially an instruction manual for practical application, then, what is it? If it's not mainly about what we need to do, what is it about? If it's not about us, who is it about?

The Bible Is about Jesus

About Jesus? "Well, *duh,*" you're thinking right now. That goes without saying.

And I agree. It has been going without saying. But we need to keep saying it. We don't "go" without saying this. The Bible is about Jesus. Front to back, page to page, Genesis 1:1 to Revelation 22:21, the written Word of God is primarily and essentially about the saving revelation of the divine Word of God.

Jesus himself said so, for instance, and here we find our first counterargument against Andy Stanley's claim that there's no biblical example of someone preaching through the Bible "verse by verse." In Luke 24, we see two of Jesus's disciples walking on the road to Emmaus and discussing the report they'd gotten of Christ's resurrection. Suddenly Jesus himself sidles up next to them. He asks them what they're talking about. They don't recognize him at first, so they explain that they are discussing the matter of Jesus, expressing their confusion about his having been given up to be crucified when all along they thought he was the one sent to redeem Israel. And they also weren't sure what to make of this astounding claim about his resurrection. Then Jesus does something very interesting: "And beginning with Moses and all the Prophets, he interpreted to them in all the Scriptures the things concerning himself" (Luke 24:27).

Basically, Jesus went through the entire Old Testament, step by step, and showed them how it all was about him. We don't have the text of his sermon reprinted for us—I wish we did!—but we can see first of all that it was expository, because it began with the books of Moses (the first five books of the Bible) and systematically proceeded through the works of the Prophets; and we can see, second, that it was self-centered, by which I mean of course *Christ*-centered. He didn't simply recite the texts; he "interpreted" them. He was preaching.

In 2 Corinthians 1:20, Paul tells us that all the biblical promises "find their Yes in him." The book of Hebrews is a great sustained example of this truth, showing us how all that led up to Christ was preaching Christ from the shadows, as it were, even reminding us that the mighty acts of the great heroes of the Old Testament were not about themselves but about acting "by faith" in the promise of the Christ to come.

Indeed, everything the Bible teaches, whether theological or practical, and everywhere it teaches, whether historical or poetical or applicational or prophetic, is meant to draw us closer to Christ, seeing him with more clarity and loving him with more of our affections. The Bible is about Jesus.

Well, this may all be good and true, but how helpful is it? Does this kind of approach to teaching and preaching—Christ-centered expository preaching—actually help people grow? Does it effect any change? Or is it simply an intellectual exercise better for a fatter mind than a fitter life?

The response of the disciples to Jesus's sermon on the way to Emmaus is intriguing. "They said to each other, 'Did not our hearts burn within us while he talked to us on the road, while he opened to us the Scriptures?'" (Luke 24:32). Something happened to them by the preaching of the Word that runs deeper than an exciting experience, truer than an inspirational feeling. Their hearts burned within them. Their affections were stirred—for Christ! And in the ensuing verses we see how this motivated them out into mission, to go and tell about Jesus.

We have a similar biblical example of life-changing expository preaching in Nehemiah 8, where Ezra and his preaching team read the entire book of the Law to the gathered people, "and they gave the sense, so that the people understood the reading" (v. 8). The result? "[A]ll the people wept as they heard the words of the Law" (v. 9). They had fallen under Spiritual conviction from the preaching. In response, Nehemiah and Ezra proclaim the time of mourning over and the day of joyous feasting ready to begin.

What had happened? They preached directly from the Word of God, the people were moved by this preaching, and the result was gospel-fueled worship.

I won't belabor the point, but I will restate it: The entire Bible is essentially about the announcement of the gospel of Jesus Christ, and this information ought to shape the way we preach, because the way we preach will shape the way our churches treat the Bible and how they will grow in the faith.

Coming to the Bible in this way, then, as if its words are better than mine, as if my words must serve to illuminate and explain its words, instead of the other way around, will require affirming that all my hard work in preparing a sermon is wasted if the sermon doesn't end up preaching Jesus as the point of human existence and reflecting that the Word of God is more powerful than my helpful tips.

This isn't cheating. It is in fact hard work, at least spiritually, because it always necessitates our dying to ourselves. The sermon prep may not take as long—thank God!—but the impulse to go first to Christ can be more difficult, and counterintuitive. We must have a stronger faith, to trust that a sermon mainly about Jesus will "help people grow" more than our set of tips will.

I will go so far as to suggest to you, actually, that not to preach Christ is not to preach a Christian sermon. If you preach from the Bible, but do not proclaim the finished work of Christ, you may as well be preaching in a Jewish synagogue or a Mormon temple. Ask yourself, as you look over your sermon outline or manuscript, "Could this message be preached in a Unitarian church?" Ask, "Did Jesus have to die and rise again for this stuff to be true?"

Getting to the understanding that the entire Bible is about Jesus is the first big step toward believing an even harder truth:

The Primary Message of the Bible Is That the Work Is Already Done

One night on the way home from small group, I listened to the guy on the local Christian radio station give a ten-minute presentation of what he had learned in church the previous day. It all boiled down to an appeal to make Jesus, in his words, our "role model." It was all very nice and inspirational.

There is indeed no better role model than Jesus. You won't find me arguing against that. And wanting Jesus for his benefits (in his gospel) but not for his cross (in our obedience) is a serious problem in Christianity. But the problem with this fellow's recollection of his pastor's sermon was that it showed no indication of actual gospel content.

It could have been delivered by the Dalai Lama. The Buddhist actor Richard Gere thinks Jesus is an awesome role model. So do many atheists. The majority of the thinking world acknowledges that Jesus is a good role model, and in fact, most of them wish Christians would act more like Jesus (or at least, more like their *perception* of Jesus).

This ought to hint at the inherent deficiency in the "Jesus as role model" message: "Be like Jesus," by itself, is not good news. At one point in his gushing review, the radio dude appealed to Christians' interest in self-help books and advice columns, but chastised them, saying, "We read all of those things, but we never think to go to the Bible for God's advice!" As if the alternative to advice from the world is more advice, just from the Bible this time.

The gospel is not good advice; it is good news.

In the attractional church, the messages are predominantly of the "life application" variety, meant to make the Christian walk seem more practical or relatable or appealing. In other words, the attractional church is big on advice. Acknowledging, of course, that much applicational preaching contains proclamation and that good proclamational preaching ought to contain application, we nevertheless ought to trend more toward the proclamation. The best preaching contains both proclamation (what God has done) and application (what we should do), but the difference in Christ-centered expository preaching is that the trust for power in application is placed in the content of the proclamation. In *Breaking the Missional Code*, Ed Stetzer and David Putnam write,

> We think that a common mistake many seeker-driven churches made early on was trying to communicate relevant messages that had little or no biblical content. It seemed that the sermons were basically explanations of common-sense wisdom, or

perhaps biblical principles, but the Bible did not set the shape or agenda of the message.

We must always remember that "consequently, faith comes from hearing the message, and the message is heard through the word of Christ" (Rom. 10:17) and "the word of God is living and active. Sharper than any double-edged sword, it penetrates even to dividing soul and spirit, joints and marrow; it judges the thoughts and attitudes of the heart" (Heb. 4:12). The Bible is not simply a tool for scriptural footnoting or common-sense wisdom.[3]

The typical applicational message tends to overemphasize our good works while a good proclamational message will emphasize God's finished work. Let's all agree: It's only bad pastors who don't want to see life change in their people. None of us *doesn't* want to help people grow. But when it comes down to *how* people grow, to what actually catalyzes people toward change in their life toward obedience and service, we reach for answers. We provide a new set each week in handy outline form, inserted right there in the bulletin. But what if all this emphasis on steps and tips isn't actually the best way to help people grow? Here are some challenging thoughts:

> The preacher must courageously and ferociously believe that transformation occurs through the interplay of God's Word and Spirit. He is simply a vessel, a broken jar of clay, spilling out before the people the water of life. The Holy Spirit always uses the revealed Word of God to open the eyes of both the unbeliever and believer to the wonders of the gospel. The preacher should not feel as if he is carrying the burden of life change; he merely carries the burden of faithful exposition and the robust proclamation of the text at hand, trusting that God's Word will never return void (Isa. 55:10–11). This is the wonder and weight of preaching.[4]

---

[3] Ed Stetzer and David Putnam, *Breaking the Missional Code: Your Church Can Become a Missionary in Your Community* (Nashville: Broadman & Holman, 2006), 95.
[4] Matt Chandler, Josh Patterson, and Eric Geiger, *Creature of the Word: The Jesus-Centered Church* (Nashville: Broadman & Holman, 2012), 123.

The essential difference between applicational preaching and proclamational preaching ultimately depends on how much the preacher wishes to make of Jesus. Do you want people to walk away thinking Jesus is a big deal? Then you have to make Jesus look like a big deal. You cannot assume that simply telling people that Jesus is a big deal will work. People don't believe what you *tell* them is important; they believe what you *show* them is important. So if in our preaching we spend most of our time emphasizing good works and then a little time saying, "But really, Jesus's work is most important," we've already shown them with our sermon imbalance what we really believe.

Proclamational preaching makes much of the gospel, believing that proclaiming the finished and sufficient work of Christ for salvation is, as Paul says, "of first importance" (1 Cor. 15:3). The applicational preacher either presupposes the gospel or relegates it to the conclusion of his message, believing that what's of most importance is exhorting the congregation to live in more Christlike ways.

To be clear (again): We should be exhorting our congregations to live in more Christlike ways. But if the emphasis of our preaching is on being more like Jesus and not on the good news of grace despite our not being able to be like Jesus, we end up actually achieving the opposite of our intent. We inadvertently become legalists, actually, because we are more concerned with works and behavior than with Christ's work on our hearts. The great irony is that, despite hoping to win the unchurched with the message of the good news, we end up enticing them with a Christian form of self-help or behavior modification, neither of which has ever saved anyone.

The proclamational preacher preaches the texts of Scripture with God as the subject and the gospel at the forefront, and he does so without shame, trusting not his words or his demeanor to win souls, but the work of the Holy Spirit.

This understanding clarifies a huge reality the attractional church must absolutely come to grips with: just because you dress casually, play edgy music, and talk a lot about grace, it doesn't mean you aren't a legalist. And in fact, it's my belief that *the self-professed "culturally relevant" churches are the chief proponents of legalism in Christianity today.* They don't think they are, because they equate legalism with stuffy fundamentalism, with rigidity and dourness, with suits and ties and organ-led hymns. They equate legalism with somber preaching of the *thou shalt nots.*

But "do" isn't any less law-minded than "don't." *Dos* and *don'ts* are just flip sides of the same legal coin. The gospel isn't "don't," but it also isn't "do"; both are merely religion.

A church that is mobilized with a gospel of "do good" might make for good PR, but the gospel of "do good" cannot really scandalize (in the Galatians 5:11 sense) a lost and broken world, because most people know how to do good without the help of Christianity. They don't need the church to act like good people, really; they need the church to point to Jesus as the only truly good person.

The attractional churches often believe they are railing against legalism and offering grace because they create culturally relevant, casual, innovative environments; because they make the message of the Bible one of practical stuff to do; and because they are cheerful and creative and take WWJD? seriously, while all the while they still don't know the power of the gospel of Christ's finished work, sufficient for salvation and fit for proclamation.

They give us instead the "gospel" of busywork. But the primary message of the Bible, as it heralds to us Jesus Christ, is that the work is already done.

Remember that the Pharisees were the religious leaders who missed the gospel because of their focus on *dos and don'ts.* Pharisaical legalism was just self-help without the cool clothes. This is why today's Pharisees aren't the concerned folks in the pews worried about their discipleship (as they are so often accused), but rather the preachers on many stages across the country whose messages are always full of helpful tips on how to get better at being a

Christian but rarely gleaming with the satisfaction of Christ. Robert Capon reminds us that *"Jesus came to raise the dead*. Not to improve the improvable, not to perfect the perfectible, not to teach the teachable, but to raise the dead."[5]

The Bible's News Is Much Better Than Its Instructions

So we want to make the Bible practical. As we've already seen, the Bible is incredibly practical. We don't have to *make* it that way. It's already that way. There are lots of practical things in it, and we do need to teach them.

But we must never teach the practical points as the main points. The practical stuff is always connected to the proclamational stuff. The "dos" can never be detached from the "done" of the finished work of Christ in the gospel, or else we run the risk of preaching the law.

Here is a good focus text to help us see what we ought to be centering our Bible preaching and teaching on:

> Now if the ministry of death, carved in letters on stone, came with such glory that the Israelites could not gaze at Moses' face because of its glory, which was being brought to an end, will not the ministry of the Spirit have even more glory? For if there was glory in the ministry of condemnation, the ministry of righteousness must far exceed it in glory. Indeed, in this case, what once had glory has come to have no glory at all, because of the glory that surpasses it. For if what was being brought to an end came with glory, much more will what is permanent have glory. (2 Cor. 3:7–11)

In this passage, Paul is recalling the giving of the tablets of the law to Moses on Mount Sinai. As Moses would go up and commune with God, the glory of the Most High was so intense that it would continue to radiate off his face when he came down. The radiant

---

[5] Robert Farrar Capon, *Between Noon and Three: Romance, Law, and the Outrage of Grace* (Grand Rapids, MI: Eerdmans, 1997), 129. Emphasis original.

glory was so intense that Moses covered his face with a veil to shield the children of Israel from the intensity.

But as stark and intense and awe-inspiring as that glory was, Paul says, it is eclipsed by the ministry of the Spirit, the ministry of righteousness, the ministry of the gospel of Jesus.

This helps us to see that the essential message of the Bible is the gospel, and that therefore the gospel needs to be central to all we say and do as a church, whether in the worship service or out. This means many of us need to wrestle with the reality that the gospel is not just for unbelievers. It is for the Christian too.

Perhaps we need to see how versatile and resilient the gospel is, how much deeper and more powerful than the *dos and don'ts* this message is. Maybe we need to see that the gospel does more than the law could ever do. It goes further than the law could ever go. If the instructions come with glory, Paul says, "will not the ministry of the Spirit have even more glory?" (v. 8).

Well, we might ask ourselves, what does the Spirit do now in and through the gospel that he didn't do then and doesn't do now in and through the law?

The law is good for what it's designed to do—it's good because it comes from God—but it cannot do what the gospel does to save and change us, and this work of the gospel is so much better than the work of the law. Where the law tells us what to do, it also reveals our inability to do it, thus condemning us. But where the gospel reveals our condemnation, it announces our freedom and forgiveness.

The foundational proof of this is in how endless the rituals of the law seemed until Christ put an end to them, in the recurring phrase of Hebrews, "once for all" (Heb. 7:27; 9:12, 26; 10:10), by becoming the sacrifice to end all sacrifices, by fulfilling every jot and tittle of the law, setting aside the ordinances and legal demands by nailing them to the cross (Col. 2:14).

The news is so much better than the instructions! It is better because the news actually saves us. "For if there was glory in the ministry of condemnation," Paul writes, "the ministry of righteousness must far exceed it in glory" (2 Cor. 3:9).

It is interesting that Paul would refer to the gospel as "the ministry of righteousness." You'd think that's what the law should be called. But the law, which demands righteousness, cannot *supply* righteousness. Instead, the gospel is the ministry of righteousness, because it announces not just the blank slate of sins wiped out but the full credit of Christ's perfect obedience credited to us!

The gospel does what the law cannot do. The law cannot give life. Its power is only for "the ministry of condemnation" (v. 9). It reveals what we must do, yes, but in doing so it also holds a measuring stick up that shows how short we will always fall.

As we look out at the world and into our churches, we think we know what will fix everything. We'll just tell them to get their act together. Thus all the instructions.

But what will really save the lost world? Let me tell you: none of our complaints against it.

What will transform the hearts of the people in your church? No amount of your nagging.

What will motivate people to real life change that begins with real heart change? Not all the helpful tips in the universe.

In fact, I would venture to say that it's very possible we may inadvertently increase the sin in our church by our inadvertent preaching of the law. It's possible, actually, that all of our emphasis on the practical has only served to make things impossible.

I'm going to tread lightly here, but I fear we vastly underestimate the spiritual damage inflicted on our churches by "how to" sermons without an explicit gospel connection. The Bible is full of practical exhortations and commands, of course, but they are always connected to the foundational and empowering truth of the finished work of Christ. When we preach a message like "Six Steps to _____" or any other "Be a Better Whatever" kind of message—where the essential proclamation is not what Christ has done but what we ought to do or need to do—we become in effect preachers of the law rather than of Christ.

And I think the Bible shows us that this kind of preaching isn't just off-center but actually does great harm, actually serves to accomplish the very opposite of its intention.

Preaching even a "positive" practical message with no gospel-centrality amounts to preaching the law. A list of things to do divorced from the "done" of the gospel is the essence of legalism. And as we have seen, the message of the law unaccompanied by and untethered from the central message of the gospel does not empower us but actually condemns us. Because besides telling us stuff to do, the law also thereby reveals our utter inability to measure up.

So a steady dose of gospel-deficient practical preaching doesn't make Christians more empowered and more effective; it actually makes them more discouraged and less empowered. Primarily because the law has no power in itself to fulfill its expectations. Paul says in Romans 8:3 (NIV), "For what the law was powerless to do because it was weakened by the flesh, God did by sending his own Son . . ."

The Bible goes further to suggest, actually, that without the gospel of Christ's finished work, the preaching of the law of works serves only to *exacerbate* disobedience. Consider Romans 5:20, where Paul says, "the law came in to increase the trespass," or Romans 7, where in verse 5 he says that the law arouses sinful passions, and then goes on to discuss the inner stalemate he faces between good things he can't do and bad things he can't stop doing.

In other words, without the saving power of the gospel, we go one of two ways in having the law preached to us: either we end up being pushed to disobey (whether from anger at the law's judgment or discouragement from our inability to keep up), or we end up thinking ourselves righteous apart from the righteousness the law really points to—that of Christ. (Don't think that wanton hedonism is the only kind of sinfulness. Self-righteous legalism is in many respects worse.) And when we preach "how to" law sermons instead of the gospel, we may end up with a bunch of well-behaved spiritual corpses. We may end up creating despair in our people, who eventually realize that all the helpful tips aren't effecting the deep heart change they really need. This is where Paul goes at the end of Romans 7, despairing of himself and launching into the wonderful gospel exposition of Romans 8.

I want you to consider whether the preaching of Christless, gospel-deficient practical sermons increases self-righteousness— because it is not focused on Christ's work but on our works. Gospel-deficient practical sermons do not make empowered, victorious Christians, but self-righteous self-sovereigns. And the self-righteous go to hell.

Romans 7:10 says the law brings death. So the preaching of practical, relevant, applicational "do" messages aimed at producing victorious Christians is fundamentally a preaching of condemnation. On the other hand, it is the proclamation of grace, oddly enough and counterintuitive though it seems, that actually trains us to obey God (Titus 2:11–12).

The stakes are extremely high.

Let us preach the practical implications and exhortations of Scripture, yes. But let us not forget that the message of Christianity is *Christ*. It is the message of the sufficiency and power of salvation by grace alone through faith alone in Christ alone. Let's not preach works, lest we increase the sinfulness of our churches and unwittingly facilitate the condemnation of the lost.

According to the Bible, only the gospel is the power for salvation (Rom. 1:16). But the gospel's power for salvation extends beyond justification, as it grounds our sanctification and glorification as well. We must stop treating the gospel as though it were power enough for a conversion experience but falls short of empowering all the practical matters of faith that come after. As Tim Keller has said, "The gospel is not the ABC's of the Christian life; it is the A to Z."

Of course, all of us are ready to confess that we are saved by God's grace received through our faith in Jesus Christ, and that this is apart from our own good works. Yet we still struggle so much in what Martin Luther calls the "muddling" of grace and law in the area of sanctification.

What helps people change and grow?

The implicit idea of the attractional church seems to be that the gospel is our entry ticket to the Christian life, but the law keeps us active once inside. But this assumption, Luther says, is "as though Christ were a workman who had begun a building and left it for Moses to finish." Paul has this to say about such a concept, in Galatians 3:3: "Are you so foolish? Having begun by the Spirit, are you now being perfected by the flesh?"

No, what the Christian church needs today in its imperfect fumbling back to the beauty of gospel-centrality is a stubborn unmuddling of law and grace. We cannot continue to position the gospel as entry-level Christianity. Sanctification and justification are "events" suggested in the golden chain of salvation (Rom. 8:30), sure, but both are equally powered by the gospel of grace.

When it comes to how we "do church," as it pertains specifically to how we teach and preach the Scriptures, we must make the same resolution Paul made: "I decided to know nothing among you except Jesus Christ and him crucified" (1 Cor. 2:2).

Don't treat the Bible as an instruction manual. Treat it as a life preserver.

5

From Watching
to Beholding

From my long time serving in the attractional church movement, I know from the inside how much thought, energy, and money go every week into pulling off the weekend service. It seemed that in some of the churches I was a part of, the church existed primarily to hold that weekend service.

For the first few years, as we tried new things and pressed the bounds of creativity and innovation with music, set pieces, and the like, the ministry was very exciting. I enjoyed writing dramas for our church (back when churches still did those), good quality pieces that rejected the churchy clichés and superficial theology and sappy emotionalism of the "skits" I'd grown up with. I wrote open-ended dramatic pieces that resonated, and little comedic vignettes that got belly laughs. The team I wrote for and acted in was asked to lead a workshop on church drama at an Innovative Church Conference in Houston. The work felt authentic and rewarding.

As a film buff, I also loved finding movie clips to be used in the worship services, little scenes that might set up the sermon series or illustrate a particular theme. In those days we worked almost exclusively from VHS, so it could be grueling work finding the right videos and the right places in the right videos and doing the editing necessary to make clips work in church.

As a preacher and teacher who also had been writing creative fiction since I was a kid, I relished trying to be creative in crafting sermons, seeing what imagery or illustrations I might use, how I might bring in pop culture references or tell effective stories.

I ate, slept, and breathed this stuff. We all did. We wanted to make an impact for Christ, and this was the way we saw it could and should be done.

The challenge to keep surprising, keep engaging, keep innovating in designing the weekend worship experience kept us busy and animated, not just physically but mentally and emotionally. So at some point, we would begin to notice signs of burnout in our volunteers. And not just of the physical kind. When someone is simply tired and needs a "breather," you can give them a break and plug more volunteers into the space they leave. In a growing church, you might be constantly replenishing your supply of able bodies and creative minds. But this burnout was more like a "checkout." It wasn't just, "I need a break." It was more along the lines of, "I'm not being fed. I'm not growing. I don't find this meaningful anymore."

Certainly volunteers and leaders in any kind of church environment can and do say things like that. But for me personally, as more people voiced not just discouragement but disillusionment, I began to question internally, "Is this right? Are we actually doing what God wants us to do? What if we've made a mistake?"

One thing that always bugged me, even while laboring toward the goal of putting on exciting worship services and other programming, was how we would describe our events and our church itself as "relevant" and "innovative" and "authentic." These and related ideas seemed to be the key concepts we used to advertise what we did. But the more we pressed into designing things just right and scheduling them just so and pursuing a level of excellence that (in our minds) rivaled the mainstream media, actually, the less authentic it felt. It seemed as though authenticity was a style we were going for, which is, surely, the exact opposite of authenticity.

Further, it began to strike me as odd that we would describe what we were doing as "innovative" when hundreds of churches across the country were doing the same thing. To this day, it kind of makes me laugh to see some churches that do "God at the Movies" series (or what have you) claim to be innovative, when they're doing what many other churches have been doing for at least twenty years now.

I also began to wonder if all this pursuit of relevance actually had the opposite effect. When my life fell apart, I found the exciting, innovative, creative, relevant worship services of my large attractional church not just irrelevant to what I was actually going through, but in some ways *harmful*. But I'm getting ahead of myself . . .

Authentic Worship

The first thing we confront is that worship in evangelical culture has become synonymous with music. I never would have intellectually assented to the notion that worship always means music, but I will never forget how pleasantly jarring it was, back in the mid-'90s while listening to a Vineyard "Winds of Worship" live album, to hear one of the leaders closing the music time and transitioning into whoever was about to preach, with the words, "We don't stop worshiping now. We keep worshiping all through the preaching of the word . . ." I wouldn't have denied that notion before hearing it, but somehow hearing it was a necessary thing.

Worship has become a bona fide movement, a cottage industry. Worship music has become a stand-alone genre. Whereas you used to have to go to church or to a worship service of some kind to hear specifically worshipful worship music, now you can go into your local bookstore and buy a recording of worship music. Up-and-coming musicians now don't have to feel called into the "ministry," and they don't necessarily have to be attached to a church as an on-staff director of worship—they can go right into a studio and be singers of worship music.

As a result, the culture of worship in the American church has enjoyed a great liberation. We can take the spirit of musical worship wherever we go. We don't have to wait until Sundays to be led into worship music. We can do it in our car, or in the gym, wherever.

On the other hand, this inundation, this popularization of worship music as a genre and as a movement, has a very real danger of becoming a fad, a trend. And what grew up out of the Jesus Movement in the '70s, the youth ministry movement of the '80s, and the recent charismatic renewal in the mid- to late-'90s (Third Wave, etc.) has resulted in an almost unconscious equating of emotionalism with worship.

You know what I'm talking about: if you grew up, as I did, in the result of a revivalist Baptist background, in the student ministry culture—in youth camps and evangelistic events—you know that if you can provoke an emotional reaction in kids, you can move them toward decisions for Jesus. Right? Play the right songs, with the right fervency, and you could get kids to give their life to Yogi Bear, if they thought it would save their hormonal souls.

But emotionalism is addictive. The danger in this is that we end up craving the emotions associated with emotional worship, not necessarily the spirit of worship itself. And as my good friend Bill Roberts, an occasional worship leader himself, once said, "The potential is always there for people to worship worship."

Things can go off the rails gradually or crazily, as more emphasis is placed on emotionalism and "freedom in worship" and less emphasis is placed on the object of worship. It becomes less about connecting with God and ascribing worth to him, and more about experiencing or enjoying a heightened feeling. We might even call this "sensuality," which is something the Bible actually forbids (Rom. 13:13).

In the late-'90s, this happened with vivid effect at the Vineyard Church in Toronto. A new outpouring of Spirit-filled worship began there and people, especially within evangelical charismatic circles, were touting it as the beginning of a revival. There were reports of healings and miracles taking place there, people were coming in the thousands, and hundreds were getting saved. Articles and books were written, journalists did news stories, advocates championed it, and critics condemned it.

For a while, what happened there looked to be very good. But there was a danger unrealized in the sort of experiences taking place, and the danger became realized. What started as spirited worship with a charismatic flavor became complete chaos. People laughing uncontrollably and then barking like dogs, roaring like lions, and clucking like chickens.[1] Men and women were flopping around on the floor in convulsions in the hundreds and walking around speaking in chaotic, discordant tongues.

I'm not a cessationist. It's not the charismata that are offensive to me, it is the complete lunacy that claims Spiritual authenticity. The spirit of such worship is not of God but of the Great Deceiver. I know some historians are trying to find the good in that movement and others like it (a similar "revival" occurred in Brownsville, Florida, a few years later[2]), but to the Bible-shaped mind and conscience, we see here the extreme example of what happens when people worship worship.

Of course, most evangelicals today aren't roaring like lions or clucking like chickens. But we are in very real danger of worshiping worship. We are in very real danger of divorcing our styles and preferences from our object.

---

[1] Vinson Synan, *The Holiness-Pentecostal Tradition: Charismatic Movements in the Twentieth Century* (Grand Rapids: Eerdmans, 1997), 275.
[2] Steve Rabey, "Revival: Brownsville Revival Rolls Onward," *Christianity Today* online (February 9, 1998), http://www.christianitytoday.com/ct/1998/february9/8t2080.html.

Those of us serious about reforming the discipleship culture of the American church must work at reforming the way the church not only does music, but more generally, the way the church *views* worship. Worship must really be worship, which is to say worship *of God*, the triune God. And this worship encompasses more than music.

What *is* worship? The problem in these emotionalistic, faddish, trendy times is that worship becomes more about us than about God. Let's look at Moses's encounter with *YHWH* in Exodus 34:5–8:

> The LORD descended in the cloud and stood with him there, and proclaimed the name of the LORD. The LORD passed before him and proclaimed, "The LORD, the LORD, a God merciful and gracious, slow to anger, and abounding in steadfast love and faithfulness, keeping steadfast love for thousands, forgiving iniquity and transgression and sin, but who will by no means clear the guilty, visiting the iniquity of the fathers on the children and the children's children, to the third and the fourth generation." And Moses quickly bowed his head toward the earth and worshiped.

The first thing to notice here is that Moses is worshiping in *the beholding of all that God is*. It's not some caricature of God or some misinformed idea of God that Moses is worshiping. It's not just one aspect of God in view. It's all of God. It's God in his fullness.

Verse 6 says it's God who is merciful and gracious. It's God who is slow to anger and who is steadfast and faithful and loving and forgiving. But verse 7 says this is also the God who is holy, who does not treat sin lightly, who allows the repercussions of sin to reverberate down through history. This is not just God the forgiver but also God the judge. It's not just the loving God; it's also the holy God. That is the whole person of God. And that is what prompts Moses to bow his head in reverence and worship.

In the subsequent verses (34:9–14) God warns Moses against idolatry. He warns Moses against directing his worship, his rever-

ence, his awe, his submission, his desires to anything or anyone
else but God. So he tells him that he will drive out these foreign
idolaters, these foreign peoples who are corrupting and compromis-
ing the holiness of God's people—the peoples whose cultures are
infecting God's community with the customs and rituals geared
toward worship of gods or objects who are not the one true living
God. He tells Moses to tear down the altars, break the pillars, cut
down the idols. Kill your idols, he says to Moses. Because *YHWH*
God is a jealous husband who will have no cheaters.

Authentic worship always begins with God.

It is important for attractional church leaders not to be allergic
to theology. Theology helps us not be sinners. A good theology of
worship helps us understand that worship begins not with asking,
"What would move people?" or "What would engage people?" but
by recognizing that authentic worship begins with God, not with
us. We have an innate desire to worship, which is why we fall into
self-worship and idolatry so easily. We are designed to worship. We
are never not worshiping. That comes from God.

So when we approach a time of worship, we should always remember that we are responding to God's call to us, reacting to the
desire that he has planted in us. Our worship is initiated by God.
See how Moses is responding to God, responding to God's calling
him into covenant. If you remember, Moses was kinda minding
his own business, having fled into the wilderness after killing the
Egyptian. And God intervenes with the burning bush. Same deal
with Paul. Just walking to Damascus, and God interrupts. The awe
and the reverence is a response to God's calling upon us.

The danger we face when we worship is coming into the experience assuming we are summoning God. Assuming worship is our
initiative. Assuming we are somehow the ones in control, that we
are bringing the best of ourselves and our holy desire to worship.
When the reality is, worship does not begin with the worshiper. It
begins with God. It is a response to God's calling upon us.

In addition, because authentic worship begins with God, it must have the real, one true living God as its object. We cannot worship the god of our preference, or the god of our pleasing. We must worship God for who he really is, not for who we'd like him to be. This means that when we come and worship, we're not just worshiping the God who is touchy-feely and lovey-dovey and "would have died for us if we'd been the only one"; we're also worshiping the God who commands storms, hangs planets, explodes galaxies, and sends people to hell. We're worshiping the God who controls the universe. We're worshiping the God who has the power and authority of all eternity. This is not your own personal Jesus. That God is manageable. No, we worship the God who is the Great I AM, the God who was and is and is to come. The God who created the universe out of nothing. The God who gives life and takes it away. The God who sends rain on barren lands and the God who is a consuming fire.

This is why *worship cannot be a-theological*. Meaning, it cannot be divorced from truth, from right belief. Worship is not just about singing and emotions and feeling a good vibe in connection with God. It must be about knowing God, and knowing who he is.

Do you remember when Jesus was speaking to the Samaritan woman at the well (John 4:1–42), and she tried to sidetrack him in his speaking about her sins by talking about worship? She was talking about worship in a ritualistic sense, in a stylized sense. Do you worship here? Or there? Where's the best place to worship, to make worship real?

And Jesus said the real worshipers worship in spirit and in truth (4:23). Authentic worship, then, pursues the spirit of worship but also the full knowledge of who God is. When we worship with right theology, with getting the God thing right, we are giving God his worth. That's what worship is—ascribing worth to someone or something. So if we say we're going to worship God, we must ascribe to him his full worth, his full glory, not simply the stuff we like most about him. Thinking about worship in this way makes some of our most popular songs seem very, very wimpy.

If you worship God in a less-than-clear or in a doctrine-less sense, you end up worshiping another god. You worship the god made in your image. When we divorce theology from worship, when we fail to cultivate a theology of worship, we compromise our worship. It may look great, but it is hollow and shallow.

Ponder this biblical phrase: "the splendor of holiness" (Ps. 29:2; 96:9). That's the sense in which we worship God—we worship him in the splendor of his holiness. That's the sense of knowing him in his fullness. He is holy. He is glorious. He is *God*. Here is one example from the Bible:

> And the four living creatures, each of them with six wings, are full of eyes all around and within, and day and night they never cease to say,
>
> > "Holy, holy, holy, is the Lord God Almighty,
> > who was and is and is to come!"
>
> And whenever the living creatures give glory and honor and thanks to him who is seated on the throne, who lives forever and ever, the twenty-four elders fall down before him who is seated on the throne and worship him who lives forever and ever. They cast their crowns before the throne, saying,
>
> > "Worthy are you, our Lord and God,
> > to receive glory and honor and power,
> > for you created all things,
> > and by your will they existed and were created."
> > (Rev. 4:8–11)

That is worship in the splendor of God's holiness. The center of worship is the perfect and eternal God—the character of the Creator, not the achievements of the created.

Some of the new church music (and some of the old) is nothing more than a celebration of how happy we are, how excited we are, how willing we are, how "worshipy" we are. We've got to gently urge our leaders to see that that is so often self-worship.

But! Self-worship in music derives from the deficient state of evangelical thought and culture in general. It's a functional ideology problem. It is, in other words, a *pulpit* problem, a pastoral problem. Self-celebratory worship music is the result of self-celebratory teaching and discipleship. So to reform worship music, we must reform our thinking about where worship begins and what it encompasses, and this will involve teaching each other and reminding each other that authentic worship is not a great thirty-minute set once a week but an entire way of being.

Day and night, the creatures in Revelation 4 never stop worshiping. They are constantly living in and believing in the splendor of God's holiness. Worship for them is not about just singing or having a time out of the week. It's day and night, never stopping.

Worship is a way of life, a quality of the believing heart. It's not just what we do; it comes from who we are. It stems from our heart, our character, not just our feelings or behaviors. It's not a going through the motions once every now and then, and it's not merely a ritual, no matter how sincere, that we do in worship services or set to music. We don't need music to worship, we just need God and a heart for him. So that everything we do—eat, sleep, breathe, play, live, work, create—is an act of worship. When we consecrate ourselves to God, when we humble ourselves before him and submit to his authority and to his will, then everything we do, 24/7, is worshiping God. Our whole life is to be a living, breathing worship service.

At the same time, even though our worship is to consume our whole life, it is meant to be self-abandoning. Look at the second part of that Revelation passage again. What did they do? They cast their crowns down before the throne. Coming before God, they reflect humility. They don't come before him with a worship that is self-involved and self-centered. They come before him in the splendor of his holiness, and he is increased while they decrease (see John 3:30).

Modern church worship is characterized by an exaltation of the self, but authentic worship is marked by an emptying of ourselves. The problem we have these days with worship is how self-involved, how humanistic it can be. From the pursuing of an emotional high to the glorification of worship leaders/singers/musicians, the act of worship becomes more and more about highlighting the act itself, or the worshiper him- or herself. This is why so much of the worship service in an attractional church strikes the outsider as a performance, a show.

But authentic worship says, "This isn't about me." Like the worshipers in this Revelation passage, authentic worship comes before God and says, "I'm not worthy."

In Hebrews 12, Christians are described as having come to the city of God for a big feast and gathering, and that gathering is all about Jesus. The mediator of the new covenant who cleanses us with his blood. And the author of Hebrews says, "See that you do not refuse him who is speaking" (12:25). The worshipers are there to celebrate the forgiveness of sins in Jesus Christ, and the warning is given: "Don't refuse this proclamation." What is that proclamation?

It is the announcement of the good news of Jesus! It is the gospel.

Real Worship Is about Beholding the Gospel

Worship is a response to the proclamation of who God is and what he has done. Specifically, Christian worship is a response with our lives to the good news of what God has done in and through his Son Jesus Christ. Authentic worship hears the proclamation, "Repent, for the kingdom of God is at hand," and says, "Yes! I want that! I need that! I submit to that!"

Authentic worship doesn't just focus on the fullness of who God is, but it glories in the beauty of what God has done. It is joyful, grateful, bathed in grace because of the wondrous, amazing grace of God in Jesus.

It is awed and overwhelmed and humbled by the awesome power of the gospel. It is moved and awed—even scandalized— by the power of the cross of Christ. Real worship, as N. T. Wright says, doesn't check its watch. It is basking in the warm glow of eternity.

Malachi 2:5 (NIV) speaks of this gospel reverence in the same way the author of Hebrews does (see Heb. 12:28): "My covenant was with him, a covenant of life and peace, and I gave them to him; this called for reverence and he revered me and stood in awe of my name."

The covenant of grace, the incredible gift of the gospel—while we were yet sinners, Christ died for us—calls for reverence, for standing in awe of the name of God. "Oh, wow, God! How can you, who are so holy and mighty and powerful and eternal and incredible, lower yourself to become a man and die an excruciating death just to bring me into relationship with you?" That's crazy. That's bewildering. That freaks me out.

The God who does that is awe-some. The God who does that provokes worship from me. "You deserve worship for who you are, but I also am moved to revere you and consider you awesome because of this staggering thing you have done for me. This covenant relationship you initiate with me through the blood of your only Son—that calls for my worship."

The gospel is a burning bush in the middle of our silent wilderness. The gospel is a blinding light interrupting our minding our own business on a lonely road. The gospel is a call to people going about their everyday, workaday lives to come and die and thereby truly live.

And when your world has been rocked by the gospel of God's grace, then your worship becomes so much more authentic, so much more heartfelt, so much more vibrant. Then it becomes the quality of your life, because you know God didn't save you just so that you could learn some tools for helpful living; he saved you from the depths of death and sin itself. He has turned your life around, given you new life, and your response must be a life lived in obedience, in submission to him.

See that you don't refuse him who is speaking! (Heb. 12:25). He's given his life; our response should be the gift of ours.

Authentic worship reflects the gospel in myriad ways, like a prism through which a great light is shone. For instance, when we gather together corporately to worship God in a worship service or in any gathering of believers, because the gospel is about reconciliation we are making a living picture of reconciliation. We are foreshadowing heaven when we gather to worship. We get, in our earthy, fallible, finite way, a taste of what it will be like when we gather together in eternal worship.

So here are the questions we must ask in whatever ways we find appropriate within our local congregation contexts:

As we gather, do we do it in a spirit of worship and truth? Do we do it with the full weight, the gravity of eternity behind it? Is it just a trendy, emotional, ritualistic behavior we do because it's just what Christians do? Or do we come, believing in the one true God, in awe of who he is and what he's done, as an outpouring of a life dedicated to worshiping him at the cost of all other idols and objects of worship, and in anticipation of the glory, the splendor, the beauty of heaven?

When we gather, are we gathering as watchers or as beholders? Are we gathering to see a performance or to see the passing by of the glory of God?

Sally Morgenthaler writes,

> We are not producing worshipers in this country. Rather, we are producing a generation of spectators, religious onlookers lacking, in many cases, any memory of a true encounter with

God, deprived of both the tangible sense of God's presence and the supernatural relationship their inmost spirits crave.[3]

I have previously suggested that the raison d'être of the attractional church is to get as many people as possible through the doors and into a worship service so that they may (ostensibly) receive information on how to have a relationship with God and then live a successful Christian life. This is a good and sincere motive, and plenty of seeker churches and their attractional worship services have seen plenty of people make decisions for Christ.

But if "what you win them with, you win them to" is true, it's possible that the Christ we offer in our excellent productions is not a full enough picture to be real. Especially if he is presented as a moral example or if he's added on to the end of a "how to" sermon. It's possible the Jesus we're winning people to isn't Jesus at all. He might actually be what my friend Ray Ortlund calls "Jesus Junior."

Actually, we should have a clue that we aren't proclaiming Jesus "in the splendor of his holiness" when we're designing our worship gathering in terms of giving people what they want. When we activate the functional ideologies of consumerism and pragmatism, we are obscuring Christ's power with faith in our own. In some sense, we are then trusting in our own glory, not in God's. We think his glory needs our producing to actually "work."

Ecclesiastes 3:11 informs us, "He has also set eternity in the human heart" (NIV). There is a gaping wound in the soul of every human being that can be filled only with something infinite. A four-step sermon and a rockin' band will not do the job.

The gospel *must* be central because nothing else even comes close to filling the eternal gap.

Once after the evening Easter service at our Nashville church plant, a guy came up to me and said, "Thank you. I can't tell you how refreshing it is to hear about the resurrection of Jesus on

---

[3] Sally Morgenthaler, "Emerging Worship," in Paul A. Basden, ed., *Exploring the Worship Spectrum: Six Views* (Grand Rapids, MI: Zondervan, 2004), 30.

Easter." I sort of laughed, figuring he was joking. But that week I listened to the sermon podcast from the church service he had attended Easter morning. He was not joking. The sermon made only passing mention of Christ's resurrection, focusing instead on how Easter is all about "new opportunities" and "walking through new doors." The power of Easter, in other words, was us.

We must not preach like that.

In years past, churches have opened Easter Sunday services with AC/DC songs, laser light shows, egg drops from helicopters, and the like. Every year there's the pressing need to outdo the previous year. How will we top ourselves? A friend who has worked in the creative departments of some of the biggest, most influential churches in America once texted me after a meeting, saying their discussion had focused on what the church could learn from Lady Gaga's ability to constantly reinvent herself, to top her last provocation with a newer one.

The simple explanation for all this ridiculousness is that we all want people to hear about Jesus! And these efforts, as silly as they seem to some, are simply ways to get people interested in church and draw them into a place where they can hear the message. But I am reminded of the time Jesus tells the rich man in hell that if his surviving family didn't believe Moses and the prophets, they weren't going to believe a resurrected man (Luke 16:31).

Does believing before seeing sound backwards to you? The same principle is at stake as we rethink the attractional paradigm. If the message that Jesus died *and came back to life* (!) isn't compelling enough to draw people, the enticement of winning a car (for example) is not going to work. Anyone who believes on Christ because they were attracted by "stuff" has been won to stuff, not Christ. That kind of winning is more like the prosperity gospel, not the biblical gospel.

Question: Why don't we trust that the gospel is itself *power*? That maybe it doesn't need our help?

It would seem, for all our massive productions and pursuit of uber-excellence, that in fact our scale of measurement is far too small. The Bible speaks to all manner of good and useful things, but mankind is starving for the glory of God. We too easily forget that the gospel fills that eternal void, that it is the division between real life and death, that God is infinite and our sin is a condemnation-worthy offense against an eternally holy God.

Every week, people file into our church services aching for eternity; in our zeal to provide something they may find comfortable and useful and inoffensive, are we offending the God who wishes to offend us in awe of his glory? Are we dismissing our brother Jesus, whose formula for victory includes crucifixion?

That should be the chief service of our worship services: *beholding*. Behold our glorious God and his lavishing of grace on us in his precious Son!

With all of this in mind, let's consider some practical advice for those charged with leading music.

Tips for Worship Leaders

First, worship leaders, ask yourself, while choosing songs and arranging a set list (and even choosing musicians), "What is the purpose of this?" You may say it is to bring people into worship of God, but everyone says that. Look at your songs, look at your arrangements, look at the people assisting you. Are they all on board with this purpose?

Second, please remember that the vast majority of your congregation is not musically savvy. They need to be able to follow where you're leading. So don't get fancy on us. If you change keys, take long pauses, run words together, change tempos, go too high or too low, or don't provide a way for those who don't know the words to know what they're singing, you may lose them. It may make for a great performance, highlighting the great skill and talent of you and your musicians, but worship is not a concert.

Third, and along those same lines, keep it simple. This does not mean *simplistic*. Contrary to popular belief, repetition is not bad. It is helpful, actually. Droning or mindless repetition is bad. But the repetition of a chorus or melody is helpful for congregants who shouldn't have to focus on keeping up with you.

Fourth, you are not a rock star. Cut it out.

Fifth, beware of banter. Good worship leaders develop sensitive and strategic ways to shepherd their people into the worship experience. This may include explaining songs or reflecting on their meanings. Maybe it means quoting or reading Scripture. It should include interspersed prayer. It could mean a lot of things, but refrain from speechifying, from lapsing into some extended pontification between songs. Save the preaching for the preacher.

And when you do banter, be mindful of what you say. Is shouting, "Are you guys ready to have fun tonight?" a good way to begin a worship set? It is not wrong or bad for worshipers to enjoy themselves in worship; indeed, they should. But is "fun" what you really want to call their attention to when you begin?

Sixth, words matter. And they matter beyond their poetic quality. What do the lyrics of the songs you're singing say about God and about the Christian life? They do not have to be systematic theology set to music, but neither should they be vapid or borderline meaningless. It may sound pretty, but does it reflect sound doctrine?

Seventh, importantly, songs that highlight the gospel message and story should be prioritized and treasured.

Eighth, the music matters more than you think and less than you think. What I mean is, not every genre or style is created equal. Just because something isn't sinful doesn't mean it's appropriate for a worship gathering. Your lyrics might be straight from Scripture, but for instance if the music is kitschy and "happy clappy," you may be condescending to your congregation. If you are using complex, moody music, you may be singing a song best suited for performance, not corporate worship. If you're using different genres simply for variety's sake, you are at cross-purposes with leading authentic worship. And be careful with taking familiar songs and changing the tune, pacing, etc. It is difficult for a congregation to feel free in worship if they feel constantly ambushed by an old song taking sudden turns. If it's not broke, don't fix it.

Ninth, be mindful that you are leading a congregation in worship, which typically and ideally means a cross-section of men and women, young and old folks, different socioeconomic classes, etc. Some, if not most, men may be uncomfortable singing about "going into the king's chamber" and kissing on Jesus. Some women may be uncomfortable singing about God smiting his enemies with furious vengeance. I think, actually, there are places in worship for both sorts of songs (just as Scripture contains all sorts of portraits of our God), but be sensitive to your congregation's needs, not necessarily to your own wants.

Tenth, don't chide worshipers for not doing what you want them to. They are not there to respond to your performance. Are they not singing loud enough, clapping heartily enough, raising their hands, or looking sufficiently "worshipful"? Lead them, don't push them. Such intra-worship nagging goes against the grain of the gospel.

Last, but most important, exalt Christ.

How We Worship Shapes Our Worship

My aim throughout this project is not simply to try to convince you that the attractional way of doing church is not as good as some other ways—I don't want to write in a reactionary way or argue for one "perfect" model—but to try to convince you that the attractional way of doing church actually accomplishes the opposite of its intention. It's not that this paradigm just isn't my style: rather, I think that it doesn't do what you really want it to do—win the lost to Christ and his gospel and disciple them into fully devoted Christ-followers. That is my concern. I want what *you* want! So I'm only hoping to show you that this way works against the vision despite all the visible success.

Christianity Today's Mark Galli writes,

When we "market," we try to make a larger audience aware of the value of exchanging a good or service. We assume both parties will benefit from the transaction. Marketing is a wonderful thing. I like to hear pitches about products I might use. I like the fact that my publishers pitch my books to a larger public. Thank God for marketing!

But there's a reason Jesus said "You shall be my witnesses," and not "You shall be my marketers" . . .

Should it surprise us that in this church-marketing era, members demand more and more from their churches, and if churches don't deliver, they take their spiritual business elsewhere? Have we ever seen an age in which church transience was such an epidemic?

Should it surprise us that in this era, pastors increasingly think of themselves as "managers," "leaders," and "CEOs" of "dynamic and growing congregations," rather than as shepherds, teachers, and servants of people who need to know God? And that preaching has become less an exposition of the gospel of Jesus' death and resurrection and more often practical lessons that offer a lot of "take-away value," presented in an efficient, friendly manner, as if we were selling cheeseburgers, fries, and a shake? . . .

Today, churches large and small (the small imitating the large) have unthinkingly adopted a marketing mentality that, it turns out, subverts rather than promotes the gospel. We inadvertently imply that the church benefits as much from the spiritual transaction as does the recipient. Marketing, by its very nature, contradicts the essence of the gospel lifestyle of Jesus, who came not to be served, but to expend his life for others—no exchange implied or expected.[4]

---

[4] Mark Galli, "Do I Have a Witness?" *Christianity Today* online (October 4, 2007), http://www.christianity today.com/ct/2007/octoberweb-only/140-42.0.html.

That is the key point: "Marketing, by its very nature, contradicts the essence of the gospel lifestyle of Jesus . . ."

But let's be as clear as possible: The problem is not so much the co-opting of cultural means to disseminate the spiritual truth. We might do that in appropriate ways as we seek to contextualize the gospel message to our culture. The problem is entirely the obscuring of spiritual truth by cultural means. What was once idealized as "church can be the place where one experiences spiritual truth" has become "church is the place where a spiritual product can be consumed."

Really, every church is discipling the people in its community. We train them, with our implicit and explicit messages, with the very rhythms of our community, to follow a certain way, to be conformed to a particular path. As we worship, we learn to worship. The values our churches operate in accordance with become implanted, ingrained—over time—in those who follow along. As Mike Cosper says, "No one decides to be consumeristic. No one decides to embrace a celebrity culture or consumer attitude, but mass culture has a way of swallowing people and institutions whole . . ."[5] He's right. The ways we worship train us to worship. The ways we worship, in fact, form our theology of worship. Maybe you've heard Marshall McLuhan's famous dictum, "The medium is the message." In the attractional model, what is truly valued is revealed by what receives the most energy, the most effort, the most "screen time." So if we worship in a consumeristic way, inserting the message of the gospel will not offset the reality that our way of worship is revealing that we really trust something else. Later Cosper writes, "How we gather shapes who we are and what we believe . . ."[6]

Let me press in on a particular example. A non-Christian named Mike comes to a worship service. The auditorium is dark and the stage is bright. The music is loud and the lyrics have a lot of first-

---

[5] Mike Cosper, *Rhythms of Grace: How the Church's Worship Tells the Story of the Gospel* (Wheaton, IL: Crossway, 2013), 16.
[6] Ibid., 94.

person pronouns, so Mike is singing mainly about what "I believe" and how "I feel." But he can't really hear himself anyway. He also can't hear the congregation singing. He is in many ways having a very personal worship experience inside his head in the middle of a crowd. The sermon is engaging and smart and based on the Bible, but its message is along the lines of putting faith into action at work in order to love your job more. When Mike goes home, he realizes he thoroughly enjoyed the service and will probably go back. He does. At some point he looks in the bulletin at the card which suggests he receive Jesus as his "personal Lord and Savior."

People can and do legitimately come to faith in experiences like this. But they also can be, and frequently are, won to an individualistic faith, a spirituality that is centered largely on themselves and their personal experiences and feelings. Christianity has been pitched as the key to self-fulfillment and personal growth. And thus a consumeristic Christian is born.

The way the attractional church worships produces the kind of worshipers it gets. And in the end, they are not the kind that the attractional church claims to want.

The Devolution Will Not Be Televised

In the middle of this discussion about the difference between worship as compartmentalized "spectating" and worship as whole-life "beholding" is the fuzzy matter of contextualization. Thus far, whenever I've written publicly against the way the attractional church idolizes excellence or strains credibility with its outsized productions, I am invariably asked what I have against technology or artistry. The answer is, nothing. At our church we have a band that plugs in their instruments. I preach through a headset mic. We have a video projector and we've used it in all kinds of ways. I am not claiming that the way we use these things is the way everyone ought to use them; I'm only trying to explain that I am not anti-technology or media or creative expression in the church.

But every one of us needs to challenge our own assumptions about these things, including the assumption that, just because they are prevalent in the culture and well accepted there, they are sanctioned for use in any way we see fit inside the church. We have to learn what being "in the world but not of it" might mean for the way we use the world's resonance with technology and media.

The attractional church's functional ideologies of consumerism and pragmatism lead to a rather uncritical use of media and technology in efforts to contextualize the message for the culture. Again, this is not an apologetic for a "traditional" church, so I am not saying you should go back to pipe organs or whatever. I'm only saying we should use these things after asking deeper questions about them than "Will this work?" It seems in some churches that anything goes so long as it is conceived creatively and executed excellently. But the uncritical use of media and technology can stunt our church's spiritual growth, even if in the short term it entertains and pleases the people.

The use of video, for instance, has become for the church just one way we've tried to reflect "where our culture's at." I don't believe video use is inappropriate in a church service, but the kinds of videos we show, the way we show them, and the extent to which we rely on them communicates a lot about our functional ideologies. We assume that the MTV generation and those who've come after need visual presentations to learn. But this assumes first of all that the purpose of the church service is to learn information and secondly that visuals actually help. Some recent research shows that PowerPoint presentations may actually hinder retention of the information presented in a talk, not help it.[7]

The uncritical co-opting of the culture's "need" for media might actually feed inside the church the negative qualities they feed

---

[7] See, for example, Alan Yu, "Physicists, Generals, and CEOs Agree: Ditch the PowerPoint," All Tech Considered blog (March 16, 2014), http://www.npr.org/blogs/alltechconsidered/2014/03/16/288796805/physicists-generals-and-ceos-agree-ditch-the-powerpoint; and Kenton Anderson, "Does PowerPoint Increase Retention?", Preaching.org (February 28, 2014), http://www.preaching.org/powerpointretention/.

outside the church: shortened attention spans, superficial imagina-
tions, inability to delay gratification, impatience with text (like the
text of the Bible, for instance), and ignorance of what to do without
constant stimulation. (It's an important spiritual rhythm to be still,
after all, and the attractional church seems to have trouble with
that.) Marva Dawn writes,

> If we always have to have everything presented to us visually,
> how can we pay attention to texts, or imagine Moses or the
> disciples, or contemplate the presence of God?
>
> The increasing speed of TV is a great contributor to the
> loss of imagination since the mind has no time to recover from
> the constant bombardment. How does this affect our ability to
> meditate on God in the necessary silences of worship? Are we
> able to deal with the ambiguities of God that force our minds
> to go beyond what is readily apparent?
>
> The loss of imagination is also related to some of the twad-
> dle (Kierkegaard's word) that characterizes some churches'
> worship these days. As William Fore explains, "Trivialization
> is inevitable in the world of the technological era, with its
> emphasis upon utilitarian means rather than truthful ends."
> If we simply want a God that "sells" to the masses, we will
> invariably reduce the truth of our multi-splendored God. If
> we want our faith to be developed as fast as problems are
> solved on sitcoms, we will not have the patience to imagine
> God's working in us to grow us when there are no immediate,
> visible results.
>
> Worship that is filled with splendor, in contrast, will greatly
> stimulate . . .[8]

There is that "splendor of holiness" idea again. The kind of
splendor Dawn is referring to is the kind that comes from the splen-
did supremacy of Christ, who is the bright morning star and the
radiance of the glory of God, as revealed by the Spirit working

---

[8] Marva J. Dawn, *A Royal "Waste" of Time: The Splendor of Worshiping God and Being Church for the World*
(Grand Rapids, MI: Eerdmans, 1999), 77.

through his written Word. But we settle for video splendor, laser splendor, flashing lights splendor. We want to dazzle with the wrong things.

The uncritical use of media, then, works at cross-purposes with what we actually hope for, for our churches. And I think this hindrance is also present in the widespread and increasing use of video preaching in church services.

Why I Think "Video Venues" Are Not a Wise Use of Technology

First, a couple of disclaimers:

My opposition to video venues is not to the multisite model for church growth generally but to the specific use of video preaching (and video music, where that is present) as the main feature of a worship gathering. There are quite a few churches that appear to do multisite well, by which I mean they feature live preaching, they have dedicated elders shepherding a community rather than organizers attracting a crowd, and they function for the most part like church plants. I think some multisite approaches are viable means of a church's gospel mission. In any event, my aversion to the video venue multisite movement is *not* morally framed. I am *not* saying video venue multisite is sinful. I am not speaking to its wrongness per se, but rather hope to suggest it is not wise. Sort of a "not everything that is permissible is profitable" kind of thing (see 1 Cor. 10:23).

Second, some of my best friends are multisite pastors. And they are all fantastic, humble, godly men who love Jesus, love the church, and love seeing lost people get saved. I am not against them.

Not to further weaken the arguments of this section with more qualifications, but in addition to those caveats I would like to acknowledge that people may oppose video venues for wrong reasons. Christopher Ash has done a good job of effectively expressing a couple of invalid reasons to disagree with video preaching:

The first is downright worldly: envy. It's never crossed anyone's mind to suggest I should preach to several congregations
via screens because, well, my preaching is not of that quality. Would that it were! As a pastor infected with the disease
of ministerial envy and pride, I can feel irritated when others' preaching is so good that people want to see *them* even
through a screen. I'm ashamed of my attitude, and I ought to
be ashamed. I write from the UK, where the Christian scene
is so small that we have (to my knowledge) no multi-campus
churches and no preachers sufficiently well-known for this
setup to be requested. So, in my perverse British (nay, English)
way, I instinctively don't like the idea. That dislike is worldly
and needs to be cleared out of the way.

The second invalid reason is cultural conservatism: I don't
like it because I'm not used to it. In the same way, I don't really
like using an electronic diary; I use one, but it feels wrong. But
this is simply because I'm getting old (in my 50s, no less, and
how geriatric in our culture) and am in danger of becoming a
cultural dinosaur. No doubt a previous generation didn't feel
the telephone was a natural instrument to use. The fact that it
doesn't feel right isn't an argument against it; indeed, it may
simply be a challenge to me to adapt and get used to it.[9]

So, all of that said, here are five reasons I would say the use of
video preaching should be discouraged:

*1. I do not think it is wise, in our consumer culture, to go down the
path of continued un-incarnation.*

This applies to the "virtual church" phenomenon in general,
as well, where Christians may attend an online worship service
all by themselves from the privacy of their own home or office.
In a day when the idolatry of the self and the mass production of
beauty and the disconnection of individuals from each other are
daily, constant, pernicious struggles, I don't think the church can

---

[9] Christopher Ash, "Why I Object to Screen Preaching," The Gospel Coalition blog (April 17, 2013), http://
thegospelcoalition.org/blogs/tgc/2013/04/17/why-i-object-to-screen-preaching/.

afford to un-incarnate anything, much less its preaching. Video is by definition un-incarnational.

2. Video venues are not countercultural.

You can go a lot of ways with this thinking, sometimes overboard, but the kingdom of God is supposed to run counter to the way of the world. What we see in the worst examples of the video venue movement is just more accommodation of cultural values begun in the modern church's idolization of relevancy. All churches should be seeker sensitive in the best sense of the phrase, meaning seeker comprehensible and seeker welcoming, and all churches should be good students of the culture and good workers at contextualization; but there is a line between contextualizing and accommodating, and I think video venues often cross the line. At what point do we look at cultural trends not as things to mirror and copy but as things to challenge and subvert? Technology *may* be neutral, as some insist, but that does not automatically mean that all technological tools are suitable for uncritical ecclesiological appropriation. I am afraid many churches have moved from leveraging technology to merely co-opting whatever they think the world finds appealing or slick.

3. Video venues can reinforce the kind of pragmatism that quenches the Holy Spirit.

The functional ideology behind video preaching is pragmatism, because it is predicated on the idea that the satellite campus is viable only if the main attraction is the speaker of the main campus. In running with this idea, it denies the idea that the power for church growth is the powerful gospel preached by qualified teachers. In other words, we have to ask, "Would this campus be successful if it had a live preacher who wasn't the main campus preacher?" And if the answer is no, doesn't that tell us something important and critical about what we're basing our growth on? Doesn't it say we are trusting something other than the gospel? And isn't this a fundamental distrust in the Spirit and a functional trust in our methods?

4. A video preacher cannot embody in the video venue the life-or-death-ness of preaching.

To put it more bluntly, a preacher on a TV screen can't be murdered.

This will sound like a morbid point to some and probably like macho posturing to others, but we know that some preachers put themselves in danger when they get up to deliver the Word of God. In the last year, a preacher in America was shot and killed in his pulpit. Certainly this isn't "good," but I do think it is a meaningful reflection of what preaching *is*.

A preacher serves his community well when he sees his proclamation of the gospel as standing before them on the spiritual precipice of heaven and hell. By doing so live and not by video feed, he incarnates the prophetic call of Scripture, reminding his flock personally of the despair of death and the eternal life of Jesus Christ. And this is driven home anytime a pastor sweats or cries on his pulpit, touches the hands of his congregation, pauses for laughter or an Amen, accommodates (or speaks over) the cries of a baby, receives the repentant and the broken for prayer and counsel, and, yes, makes allowances for safety. I hope to never send a video in place of myself, because a video cannot be shot in the face for proclaiming Jesus.

Jesus gave us, for all time, the written revelation of redemption through sacrifice and servanthood, but he still saw fit to show up in person to die.

5. Video venues assist the idolization of and overreliance on preachers.

A cult of personality is possible in any kind of church, no doubt. But when you blow the main guy's face up onto a huge screen and build an entire campus around it, the cult has become a bona fide franchise. What happens if the pastor gets hit by a bus? What happens to the other men in your church with preaching gifts? Where do they go to exercise their gifts and bless their church family?

Granted, God raises up certain men of unusual anointing to lead in unique and higher-profile ways. But what does it say about the gospel if, where the rubber meets the road, we minister as if the message requires a certain level of homiletical talent to do its work?

At any rate, I trust that these cautions are good grounds to ask probing questions, to challenge our assumption that "if it works, we should work it."

Matt Chandler, whose own face is blown up on video screens at The Village Church's multiple satellite campuses, has given us a good example of humility and bravery in publicly expressing his own concerns about the methodology. He writes,

> [A]fter studying the issue, we decided to go multi-site. Yet we still have some serious concerns and questions about the multi-site idea even as we participate in it. The problem that haunts us is a simple one. Where does this idea lead? Where does this end? Twenty years from now are there fifteen preachers in the United States?
>
> We have other questions, too. Is multi-site ministry a legitimate use of technology or an illegitimate one? Will the multi-site idea weaken the church at large by squashing the diversity of teachers, ideas, and leaders in the west?[10]

Matt is asking the right questions, and it's a credit to him and his church that they have not adopted their methods uncritically, assuming that they *should* do something just because they can.

What We Behold, We Become

There's a great scene in the '80s teen comedy *Real Genius* that is apropos of our impersonal, media-saturated times. Throughout the movie, which takes place on a university campus, the lead character attends a particular class where students are using tape record-

---

[10] Matt Chandler, "Clouds on the Horizon," 9 Marks Journal (May–June 2009), http://www.9marks.org /journal/clouds-horizon.

ers to record the professor's lecture. Each time we see him in this class, there are fewer students and more tape recorders in their place. Eventually he enters the room and finds himself alone; every desk is occupied by a tape recorder. In the final scene in this sequence, not only are the pupils' desks loaded with tape recorders recording the lecture, the professor's desk has a large tape player on it, playing the lecture. It's a funny buildup to a very sobering truth. Eventually, our relational community becomes endangered by our artificial messages and artificial receivers. We already have become this way virtually with the way we experience "community" over e-mail, text, Facebook, or Twitter. Are we heading to the day when a worship service is simply someone pressing Play on the worship band avatars and the sermon video, while the congregation "attends" via hologram?

In 2 Corinthians 3:18, Paul says that it is by beholding the glory of Christ that we are transformed "from one degree of glory to another." There is something about beholding Jesus "in the splendor of his holiness" that actually changes us. Beholding is becoming, in other words.

If we want our churches to develop into communities of fully devoted followers of Christ, on mission, that's what we must hold up for them to behold. We cannot expect our people to grow in God's glory if we do not put God's glory before their faces.

As noted previously, Vermont, where I live and pastor, is the least churched and least religious state in the nation. We are one of the six New England states, which all rank in the bottom ten in terms of religious participation and interest per capita. Our region of the country contains the highest concentration of "nones"— those who designate "none" among their options for religious affiliation. For many in our area, the times of Christian vibrancy are over. The days of deadness and dryness have long settled in. But there was a time when New England was the hotbed of evangelical fervor in the country.

When we look back at the spiritual heyday of this now-barren land, when we seek to discover just what men like Jonathan Edwards and George Whitefield were doing back then in Massachusetts and beyond to stir the Great Awakening and all its wonderful fallout, we do not see a focus on ministerial skill or ecclesiological genius. The descriptions of the religious landscape of New England back then, before the Spirit brought revival, read very similarly to the descriptions of the state of New England today. It was not a region full of decently religious people who just needed a kick in the pants. True hearts for God were few and far between. But when things began to change, suddenly and dramatically, it was not the result of a well-orchestrated strategy of church programming and evangelistic events. Instead, men like Edwards preached. And they preached big. They preached boldly. And their message was not of a particular kind of church but a particular kind of glory—the risen, beautiful, supreme, sovereign Christ Jesus in the splendor of his holiness. And the atmosphere of the place changed. The dry bones came to life.

This is what our churches need today. We cannot settle for success. Our people need real glory, and only the gospel "of first importance" reveals it.

6

Biting Off More
Than You Can Chew

I am convinced that, in the beginning of many church planting efforts, the movement stalls by and large because the church is trying to do too much. In order to launch with an appealing presence in the community, an entire range of programs and ministries are laid out from the ground level. But the churches that gain some traction and begin to grow rarely curtail what has already been installed and deemed valuable from the beginning. In other words, the bigger an attractional church becomes, the more programs and ministries it thinks it must offer.

This will be the problem of any church that sees itself as necessarily a provider of goods and resources. I remember sitting in a planning meeting for one of our previous churches where the discussion was about launching a public park on the church grounds that would include a community center inside the building for ongoing education—classes on finances and family budgeting, car repair, cooking, home computing, etc. These were great ideas, actually, and no one had a problem with these initiatives at the conceptual level. But I remember thinking about all the other things our church was already doing and how we were actually in the midst of some concern about losing volunteers of our current ministries to burnout and general disillusionment with our direction. (We had recently hired a new pastor, which typically attracts some folks but also loses others.) I thought to myself, "I wonder if we're trying to do too much."

One huge problem with accumulating programs and ministries in a church is that it adds to the institutionalization of these very programs and ministries. Hearts get attached to these initiatives; volunteers take them personally and invest lots of time and energy. Any pastor who's had to "fire" volunteers or discontinue a very old but ineffective program will know what I'm talking about. It is much easier to add programs than discontinue them, especially after they've outlived their viability.

The drive to provide an array of goods and services prevents a church from exercising missional nimbleness. The bigger the selection of offerings, the more bloated and ineffective a church will actually be. That's the cruel irony of program accumulation—it offers a way to meet many needs and reach many people, but it actually dissipates a church's missional effectiveness in a community. This happens primarily because people get confused by the menu of opportunities and about what's of greatest value, both to the church and in life in general.

A church in which I was previously involved revamped its small group programming almost every couple of years. The emphasis in one phase was on demographics, with groups structured according to age, gender, and marital status. The next phase was about promoting a church initiative, so groups were formed around the purpose of studying a particular topic the church leadership wanted everyone to focus on. The last phase I remember was all about affinity, so groups were formed around any topic or interest a leader felt compelled to provide. I remember looking through the catalog of group listings for the new season. There were small groups oriented around hiking, yoga, softball, computer games, and even brush-hogging. There was even a drum circle group. I didn't know what that was, but I doubted it was even Christian! (I'm kidding. But just kind of.) In the midst of this vast array of group listings, there were just two Bible studies. Just two.

Now, tell me, what do you think a visitor perusing this catalog would think our church valued? You might say "community," and of course that's not a bad thing in and of itself. But you certainly couldn't say "God's Word." You couldn't say "the gospel." In fact, it would be difficult to say anything definitive about our church's vision and mission except that we were pretty flexible.

And yet, that phase of small groups based on affinities eventually fizzled too. Apparently, the one affinity our church didn't have was the one thing that might have been assumed from the catalog itself: community.

Many of the leaders who decry the institutionalizing of the church do not realize they have been erecting and rapidly continue to erect institutions of their own. Programs, strategies, processes, events, etc., all contribute to whatever institutional entity your church is becoming and will become. Many are finding, too late to avoid a mess, that the life of their church is glutted with activities, patterns of activities, and accompanying information that distracts congregants and competes with the stuff that matters most.

Tony Morgan once discussed, based on the experience of the position he held at the time at Newspring Church in Anderson, South Carolina, the confusion that may happen when a church begins "sub-branding" within its programming:

> In Church world, though, *we've fallen into the trap of letting every ministry compete against each other for attention.* That's why we feel like we need to create a logo and a name for every ministry that exists in our churches. (There are some big, visible churches that have fallen into this trap.)
>
> Here are the consequences of that decision. The staff leaders end up spending an inordinate amount of their time trying

to *promote* their ministry ahead of the other ministries in the church instead of *leading* their ministry. Secondly, the people who are trying to make connections in our churches get bombarded with competing messages. From their perspective, it sounds like the ministries are shouting to get their attention and all we're doing is adding noise to people's already hectic lives.[1]

So if this kind of energy-diffusion and congregant-confusion is the result of these approaches to programming, why do we do them? The answer is that, mainly, we think we have to. We think it is the only way to attract people, please people, and grow people. We have bought into the functional ideologies of consumerism and pragmatism, which makes us do silly things like naming our ministries very culturally specific things that will sound lame ten years from now (really, Ignite and Fuse are just this generation's JAM and RAD). But the problem isn't with what we name stuff but that we have so much stinkin' stuff to name.

In his blog post, Morgan offers up the work of LifeChurch (a multisite church based in Oklahoma City but with eighteen satellite campuses across five states) as an example of good sub-branding, because instead of getting overly creative with their different ministries, they, like Google, simply add their name to the plain identification of the ministry offering: LifeKids, LifeGroups, and so on. This is smart, definitely, but there's something else Life-Church does that is distinctly admirable, and it's that they don't do too much.

As you can probably imagine, I am not a big admirer of the way churches like LifeChurch and Newspring do ministry, but this doesn't mean I can't learn good and wise things from them or their leaders (as I hope they can learn from those coming from my perspective). One of those things is the "simple church" concept,

---

[1] Tony Morgan, "Your Branding Sucks: The Sequel," Tony Morgan Live blog (March 31, 2008), http://tony morganlive.com/2008/03/31/your-branding-sucks-the-sequel/. Emphasis original. The "Jared" he mentions in the beginning of the post is not I, by the way.

which LifeChurch prioritizes for the sake of their ministry effectiveness. Here's pastor Craig Groeschel explaining the why of their
narrowed focus:

> When we started LifeChurch.tv eleven years ago, I always felt
> like we weren't a "real" church. To me, real churches had per-
> manent buildings, VBS, Christmas programs, choirs, women's
> ministries, etc.
>
> Before long, we started trying to do everything "real"
> churches do. Yet many of these activities didn't bring people
> to Christ, help those in need, or foster genuine Christ-centered
> community.
>
> Instead of adding ministries, we started cutting some:
>
> - We stopped doing church sponsored *sports*. Why take be-
>   lievers out of corporate leagues to put them together in
>   Christian leagues?
> - We stopped *VBS* because we reached more kids for
>   Christ each weekend than we did during VBS (and
>   with a lot less money and effort).
> - We stopped doing *concerts* because we were basically
>   providing entertainment for Christians.
> - We stopped doing *dozens* of other things that Jesus
>   never did but almost every church in America wants
>   to do.
>
> (I am not against these things. Your ministry might do one or
> more of these things exceptionally well and reach people with
> them. But we weren't.)
>
> We decided to focus on what we could do best to reach
> people:
>
> - Weekend Experiences
> - Life Groups
> - Missions
> - Kids
> - Youth

Maybe instead of adding ministries you might consider pruning the vine![2]

Groeschel has hit on the genius of the "simple church" model. The more bloat you cut from a church's system, the more powerful and effective it will be at carrying out its primary mission. The more bloat you cut from a church's system, the less "institutional" (in the negative sense of the word) it will be.

The Simple Church Is Simple

Many of us believe the evangelical church in America requires a radical reformation of means and methods, and as more and more churches recalibrate their visions of what it means to be the church, more and more are reevaluating the assumptions and values that have carried them thus far.

Obviously, though, we cannot dispense with church structure and authority. Some critics today are challenging the very idea of the institutional church, but that's not only naive, it's unbiblical. As Eugene Peterson says, "What other church is there besides institutional?"[3] Clearly, from the organizational outlines of the tribes of Israel to the networked churches under the apostles in the New Testament, ecclesiological anarchy is not the answer.

Setting aside the mostly "emergent" notions of abandoning defined church structures, we now set our minds to ask how a structured church, especially one that is growing, might remain a place of internal freedom and external mission.

I have characterized the attractional church's motivation as wanting to get as many people through the doors of the church building as possible so that as many as possible may learn what it means to have a relationship with God. Because this aim is somewhat broad, hoping to attract as many people as possible, the

---

[2] Craig Groeschel, "Don't Do It All, Part Four," LifeChurch.tv Swerve blog (February 15, 2007), http://swerve .lifechurch.tv/2007/02/15/dont-do-it-all-part-four/. Emphasis original.
[3] Mark Galli, "Spirituality for All the Wrong Reasons," *Christianity Today* online (March 4, 2005), http:// www.christianitytoday.com/ct/2005/march/26.42.html.

means to the end are practically endless. There are lots of different types of people out there, an increasingly diverse consumer base, so the number of goods and services the attractional church wants to offer to woo them is ever increasing as well. You can see, then, how a seeker-focused church might become exceedingly complex.

The attractional church increases its programs, its classes, its opportunities. It builds up multiplying teams with volunteers and leaders. It seeks to be a many-armed machine so that it might reach more and more people.

The worship service itself becomes increasingly complex to continue impressing and attracting congregants. Video elements, music features, lighting and sound, computer graphics, creative transitions. Such a creative machine requires lots and lots of work, lots and lots of energy, and lots and lots of volunteers.

There is a lot going on in the attractional church, more and more all the time, so the structure and the operations get more complicated all the time. But the ironic little secret, actually, is that you might reach more by doing *less*.

With less to do, we can better focus on the things that are most important. In other words, we can do a lot of things in a mediocre way, with divided interests and energies; or we can do a few things really well, with a unified vision and passion.

This difference may be directly reflective of the way most attractional churches approach missions and evangelism. The attractional church sees evangelism mainly happening inside the church building, so the attractional attempts are myriad and always increasing. A simple church may also emphasize "inside evangelism," but in cutting the programmatic bloat they also free up their people during the week to engage their neighbors outside the church. The ideal situation is that the worship gathering reflect the biblical paradigm, which in my opinion disqualifies the common "seeker service," but we'll set that aside for the moment. The main point is the simplicity that liberates as opposed to the complexity that preoccupies.

The simple church is simple. You can more easily identify what is important in a simple church. And if a church will start off simple and doggedly persist in the value of simplicity, it may remain missionally effective and motivated for years and years to come.

Simple Churches Simplify the Vision

Churches passionate about simplicity will pursue a simple vision. This doesn't mean the vision is simpleminded or puny. It just means the vision isn't multilayered, vague, or connected to numerous other pieces (mission statements, values statements, purpose statements, etc.).

Even the "purpose-driven church" gets bloated. Because the attractional church often has so much going on, with lots of programs and leadership and volunteers, it is a bigger and more unwieldy ship to steer. It is a heavy machine with lots of working parts. It therefore becomes more difficult to change or transform, and it makes ministers more unyielding and unlikely to consider changing directions. Too much time, money, and manpower has been invested in the bigness.

The narrowed structure of the simple church, on the other hand, allows great flexibility. It is easier to add or subtract, to rework and rethink, when there is not much going on structurally to begin with. Consider the calendar of activities of the average attractional church. The attractional church is a lot busier *doing*, but a simple church may be a lot busier *living*.

The attractional church develops an establishment around its goods and services and the programs designed to provide them. Challenges to rethink are taken as challenges to the establishment of the church itself. The simple church may operate much more organically. Its needs for growth are fewer and less contrived.

Sometimes the attractional church is simply chugging along in its complexity. It does things because they can be done, not necessarily because they should be done. The attractional church often reasons according to available resources (volunteers and money and building space), not according to actual spiritual value. If something is considered valuable to a valuable part of the customer base, it is deemed valuable.

I remember getting blank stares when asked what our official mission statement for our church plant in Nashville should be. I said I didn't think we needed one, and that formulating one was a waste of time. Of course, I was eventually convinced otherwise, and we eventually formulated one, and it served us well when having to reinforce What It Is We're Doing and Why. But in practice, I have seen far too many vision/mission/purpose statements that didn't go any deeper than the church bulletin, to think that these statements are all they're cracked up to be. One of the pillars of modern ecclesiology that Thom Rainer and Eric Geiger deconstruct early on in their book *Simple Church* is the indiscriminate borrowing of successful "models," as if church programs are all plug-and-playable. And one reasoning behind their targeting of this practice is just how thoughtless and unreflective it often is. Speaking to the Statement Glut problem in a highly stylized church system, using a fictitious example, they write,

> Most churches have a lot of information to communicate, but First Church also has a lot of statements. There is a mission statement, a purpose statement, a vision statement, and a strategy statement. Each statement is different from the other. And long.
>
> Looking more at the brochures, we notice that each ministry department also has different statements. Each statement is intended to describe the focus or direction of the church. There are more than ten different statements on the materials we are reviewing.
>
> What does it mean?
>
> The mission statement listed in the bulletin is "to lead unsaved people to become fully devoted followers of Christ." Obviously, someone has been influenced by the ministry of Willow Creek. The purpose statement printed on the church brochure

features five "M" words: *Magnification, Multiplication, Maturity, Ministry,* and *Mission.* Some leader had been impacted by Rick Warren and the purpose-driven movement. The vision statement highlighted on the church stationery is "loving this community to Christ." Or maybe that is the strategic statement.

Nevertheless, it was *another* statement.

It would be easier to memorize the book of James than to memorize all the statements . . . and much more profitable.

Do the statements have anything to do with one another? Are they reflected in how the church actually does ministry? Or are they just placed on top of an existing paradigm and structure? The confusion with the multiple statements indicates that there may be a multiplicity of ministry philosophies and approaches existing in the same place. It is especially unclear how all these statements fit together.

We are unsure of the real focus of the church.[4]

Rainer and Geiger contrast this example with another imagined example, interviewing the theoretical pastor of Cross Church, whose mission statement is "Love God, love others, serve the world":

"So, that is your purpose, right?"

"I guess you could say that."

"Talk to us about your process. How do you make your purpose happen?"

"Love God, serve others, serve the world is our process."

"I thought you said it was your purpose."

"It is both. Our purpose is a process."

"Oh."

Interesting. Genius. Simple.[5]

And clever. That *what* and *how* are merged is great, but obviously there are strategic implementations of programs or whatever

---

[4] Thom S. Rainer and Eric Geiger, *Simple Church: Returning to God's Process for Making Disciples* (Nashville: Broadman & Holman, 2006), 34–35. Emphasis original.
[5] Ibid., 38.

they do to *do* the *how*, the same way the Statement Glut church would say their programs were how they implement their *how*.

Nevertheless, the thinking behind this juxtaposition is great. It makes us think; it spurs us toward being deliberate, reflective, thoughtful. It inspires us not to indiscriminately borrow either programs or jargon, but to realize that no amount of sloganeering or busywork will grow our churches spiritually.

Flashing back to my vision statement aversion with our Nashville church plant, I realize the philosophical breakdown came from my fear of doing things just because "that's how you're supposed to do it." The request for a statement was well meant. My reaction was based on a fear of becoming just another ministry that indiscriminately adopts. In a day when most churchgoers couldn't tell you what their church's mission statement is (or what it means), my hope is that churches can begin to depend on their congregants' passion for the glory of God, not on their subscription to a well-turned phrase.

And I am not inclined to think that our vision ought to be so malleable, anyway. Not all visions are created equal. To further simplify the simple church paradigm, I would encourage rethinking the common allusion to Proverbs 29:18. Too many of us misinterpret the verse to allow *any* spiritual vision from a lead pastor with big thoughts. But it isn't more entrepreneurial visionaries we really need but more cross-focused visionaries. D. A. Carson says, "We depend on plans, programs, vision statements—but somewhere along the way we have succumbed to the temptation to displace the foolishness of the cross with the wisdom of strategic planning."[6]

That should remind us of the apostle Paul's "vision statement": "For I decided to know nothing among you except Jesus Christ and him crucified" (1 Cor. 2:2).

---

[6] D. A. Carson, *The Cross and Christian Ministry: Leadership Lessons from 1 Corinthians* (Grand Rapids, MI: Baker, 1993), 26.

The Simple Church Is More Nimble

Nearly every evangelical, when pressed, would insist that the church is people, not a place. A building is not a church. A set of programs is not a church. A structure is not a church. Christians together are the church. A local church is a local community of Christians covenanting together under the biblical pattern of sacraments, fellowship, discipleship, authority, and mission.

But surely this is harder to say with integrity in the bloated attractional church. (Please note again, I am not saying the *big* attractional church. Bloated attractional churches may be any size. I just think that the smaller the church, the easier it is to pursue simplicity, for some reasons that are obvious and for some reasons that are not.) If the church is people, then the organizational machine in a local congregation should be considered expendable. The organization may dissolve but the church will remain, so long as the Spirit indwells his people.

Yet many of those doing the attractional model are very fearful of the organization dissolving. There are personal visions and aspirations at stake; there is money at stake; there are buildings involved; there are lots of programs that are considered successful. The enterprise is predicated upon the longevity, the bigness, the success of the enterprise.

The divide is illustrated even in the way these congregations multiply. A simple church can be more passionate about church planting, because a simpler church is easier to replicate and because it is seen as more preferable to send a growing number of people out to start a new work than to face the difficulty of accommodating more people in the original community. (This doesn't mean the simple church doesn't value the new people who come! It only means that they do not value institutional expansion as much as they value missional expansion.) The attractional church is evidently and increasingly passionate about satellite campuses, video venues, church branding and the leadership's platforms in the public, "strategic partnerships," and the like. When an attractional church multiplies, the results more resemble franchises than church plants.

Attractional churches often believe they have something unique, something marketable, something within their organizational machine or presentation that can be sold, shared, or otherwise disseminated in order to expand the reputation, influence—again, *the brand*—of the local church name and structure. When this happens, it puts more and more of a stake in the organization itself. The church is seen as synonymous with the organization, the name, the leaders, the production. Much is done, therefore, to keep this enterprise running and growing.

But a simple church sees all that will pass away in the age to come as expendable in the here and now.

As the attractional church accumulates more complexity, it becomes more rigid, despite all its claims to innovation and cultural relevance. And as more programmatic development takes place, the more inwardly focused the church must necessarily become. Compare the budgets of large attractional churches. How much is often dedicated to outward ministry, and how much, by contrast, goes to personnel, marketing, and overhead? That a church could, as a recent example, spend more than $200,000 marketing the pastor's latest book says a lot about which basket its eggs are in. That is a huge investment in the platform of the lead guy. The church has itself become synonymous with the pastor's leadership, his voice, his personal "brand." That is one of the hallmarks of the ever-complicating attractional church.

The simple church, on the other hand, while still maintaining biblical order and structure, is freer and more agile in its attempts to treat the congregation like a body, not a machine. It has different means of measurement, different gauges of success. As the attractional church is overtaken by the business model, where quantifiable results are expected in short periods of time, the simple church adopts an approach to church growth that is more reflective of farming, of cultivation. While the attractional church expects its proven methods and powerful programs to produce results, the simple church focuses simply on the long-term investments in growth and trusts the Spirit to produce growth in his time.

The simple church follows the direction not of the shifting winds of the culture but of the surprising currents of the Spirit. Its attention is not first to the newspaper but to the gospel. Therefore, it is able to cast off that which entangles it, even the religious nets of its own devising for the fishing for men, and follow Christ wherever he may go. The simple church is missionally much more nimble than the attractional church.

Why You Should Under-Program Your Church

Having hopefully established the value of church simplification, here are ten further thoughts to reiterate and elaborate on the concept of under-programming:

1. You can do a lot of things in a mediocre way, or you can do a few things extremely well.

The over-programmed church struggles with the pursuit of excellence because its energy and focus are so scattershot. Do you remember when McDonald's offered pizza? I do, but I'd rather not. They realized pretty quickly they ought to stick to the classic McDonald's fare. They could not pull off pizza like restaurants dedicated to pizza could. Similarly, the church needs to stick to what the Bible actually tells us to do, and what the Bible actually tells us to do is not very complicated. It's difficult, sure. But not complicated.

2. Over-programming creates an illusion of fruitfulness that may just be busyness.

A bustling crowd may not be spiritually changed or engaged

in mission at all. And as our flesh cries out for works, many times filling our programs with eager, even servant-minded people is a way to appeal to self-righteousness. Like those breathless bones rustling about in Ezekiel 37, the activity may signal a life that isn't real. An over-programmed church creates an illusion of fruitfulness that belies reality.

3. *Over-programming is a detriment to single-mindedness in a community.*

If we're all busy engaging our interests in and pursuits of different things, we will have a harder time enjoying the "one accord" prescribed by the New Testament. The continued compartmentalization and segmenting of the church is not healthy either. It is harder to be the church when we are sequestered out into programs or groups centered on specific demographics or interests. If we can't engage in mission with brothers and sisters who may not share our age, social status, or personal hobbies and interests, we miss out on the important enjoyment together of the Christ we have in common.

4. *Over-programming runs the risk of turning a church into a host of extracurricular activities, mirroring the "type A family" mode of suburban achievers.*

The church can become a grocery store or merely a more spiritual YMCA—perfect for people who want religious activities on their calendar. The more we turn the church into a provider of goods and services, the more we aid and abet the consumeristic spirituality of our congregation, and the more we feed their self-righteous moralism and their relegating of their faith to a "to do" item in their weekly schedule.

5. *Over-programming dilutes actual ministry effectiveness.*

It can overextend leaders, increase administration, tax the time of church members, and sap financial and material resources from churches.

6. Over-programming leads to segmentation among ages, life stages, and affinities, which can create divisions in a church body.

Certainly there are legitimate reasons for gathering according to "likenesses," but many times increasing the number of programs means increasing the ways and frequencies of these separations. Pervasive segmentation is not good for church unity or spiritual growth. It also tempts a church to begin catering to a particular demographic as more valuable than others, determining that market share among demographics with cultural currency (or actual currency!) is preferable to ministry among other groups. This kind of thinking is antithetical to that of Christ's mission to the least, last, and lost.

7. Over-programming stifles mission.

The more we are engaged within the four walls of the church or simply within the "walls" of a church program, the less we are engaged in being salt and light. Over-programming reduces access to and opportunities with my neighbors.

8. Over-programming reduces margin in the lives of church members.

It's a fast track to burnout for both volunteers and attendees, and it implicitly pushes out Sabbath rest.

9. Over-programming gets a church further away from the New Testament vision of the local church.

Here's a good test: take a look at a typical over-programmed church's calendar and see how many of the activities resemble things seen in the New Testament. This doesn't mean that every extrabiblical program is an invalid expression of biblical commands and expectations. But many are. And many of the ones that aren't, serve largely as distractions from the few things the Bible actually calls us to do.

10. Over-programming is usually the result of unself-reflective reflex reactions to perceived needs, and an inability to kill sacred cows that are actually already dead.

Always ask "Should we?" before you ask "Can we?" Always ask "Will this please God?" before you ask "Will this please our people?" Always ask "Will this meet a need?" before you ask "Will this meet a demand?"

As in all things, every church needs someone in the room where the thinking caps are kept, with the authorization to say, "That's not a good idea."

And while y'all are in that room, let that guy take up the thinking caps and hand out the shepherds' staffs.

7

Pastoring Hearts

Like many young men starting in ministry, I began my training for pastoral work in the role of youth minister. The evangelical youth group culture of the '90s is where I cut my teeth learning how to write sermons, plan events, and manage a ministry. One thing that wasn't really taught, however, was how to disciple someone, counsel someone, or, you know, actually be with people. The closest my training came to what is really the heart of pastoral ministry was in learning how to consider the "felt needs" of the unchurched.

As I progressed in student ministry, I spent most of my time reading and writing and thinking about programs—all of which are very important practices for pastoral ministry—but realized in the few times of ministering to a personal crisis that there was something different about that work, something less mathematical and more . . . I don't know, maybe *real*? Not that studying and prayer and preaching aren't real. It was just that the time I had to confront a guy who had weed on him while he was doing his community service at the church for getting busted with weed at school, or the time I sat with a young biracial kid who was venting out the frustrations of his "trying to be black" at a majority white school when his mom was white and his African American dad didn't want anything to do with him, put me in a position of, moment by moment, not knowing what to do or say.

I know just what to do with a book in my hand. With a pen and paper, or with Word on my laptop, I seem to have little trouble coming up with ideas. But venturing into the middle of someone's pain with them, holding their hand physically or spiritually, listening to their story, praying with them, offering biblical counsel, knowing how to be both a leader and a friend, knowing when to give words and when to simply lend an ear . . . that's the hard work that necessitates wisdom, discernment, the kinds of Spiritual fruit that come with time and experience and having been deeply wounded oneself.

But that's the stuff of pastoral ministry.

And it is the stuff that seems most expendable in today's ministry-industrial complex. The higher up one climbs on the ministry career ladder, the further away it seems he gets from the people he's called to shepherd. Many are the pastors who like shepherding from their offices or their pulpits or their blog and Twitter feeds. The guys who get up close and personal on a regular basis, who don't pastor just the staff but the laity as well, don't seem to get the book deals or speaking engagements, so in the current evangelical economy of ideas we don't value their input very much. There's more cachet in being the Pastor of Vision and Preaching. But there is more biblical foundation for simply being a pastor.

What exactly is the pastoral responsibility, anyway? Is the pastoral "idea man" really a biblical vocation?

When Willow Creek copped to their mistakes, many of us wondered where the church and all its emulators would go from there. Bill Hybels and company had been bravely honest about their mistakes; what would their recovery process look like? They discovered a lack of health. What was the prescription going forward? We read things like this in *Christianity Today*:

> So what happens when leaders of Willow Creek stand up and say, "We made a mistake"?
> Not long ago Willow released its findings from a multiple year qualitative study of its ministry. Basically, they wanted to

know what programs and activities of the church were actually helping people mature spiritually and which were not. The results were published in a book, *Reveal: Where Are You?*, coauthored by Greg Hawkins, executive pastor of Willow Creek. Hybels called the findings "earth shaking," "ground breaking," and "mind blowing."

. . . [Hawkins says], "Participation is a big deal. We believe the more people participating in these sets of activities, with higher levels of frequency, it will produce disciples of Christ." This has been Willow's philosophy of ministry in a nutshell. The church creates programs/activities. People participate in these activities. The outcome is spiritual maturity. In a moment of stinging honesty Hawkins says, "I know it might sound crazy but that's how we do it in churches. We measure levels of participation."

Having put all of their eggs into the program-driven church basket, you can understand their shock when the research revealed that "Increasing levels of participation in these sets of activities does NOT predict whether someone's becoming more of a disciple of Christ. It does NOT predict whether they love God more or they love people more."

Speaking at the Leadership Summit, Hybels summarized the findings this way.

> Some of the stuff that we have put millions of dollars into thinking it would really help our people grow and develop spiritually, when the data actually came back, it wasn't helping people that much. Other things that we didn't put that much money into and didn't put much staff against is stuff our people are crying out for.

Having spent thirty years creating and promoting a multi-million dollar organization driven by programs and measuring participation, and convincing other church leaders to do the same, you can see why Hybels called this research "the wake up call" of his adult life.[1]

---

[1] "Willow Creek Repents?," Leadership Journal Parse blog (October 18, 2007), http://www.christianitytoday.com/parse/2007/october/willow-creek-repents.html.

My assumption for years, actually, has been that Willow Creek has been one of the few attractional churches that have been doing an awful lot right, especially in terms of discipleship. When the team from my church attended the Willow leadership conference in 1996, most of us were pretty surprised at just how "churchy" the place seemed to be. Yes, it was bigger than any church we'd ever seen before. We were taken aback by the food court and the enormous bookstore, but we found the advice and even the worship service itself less "innovative" than we'd expected. And as friends of ours have attended and worked at Willow Creek over the years, I've heard voices from the inside help me work against my cynicism and critical perspective about the church. So I had really high hopes not only about how the "REVEAL" wake-up call might result in a healthy reorientation around the gospel and its implications but how Willow's reorienting might "trickle down" to the reorienting of its countless imitators.

I think that fundamentally what the REVEAL survey shows us, from all the churches that participated in it, including one of my own, is twofold:

1) the attractional worship paradigm can attract the unchurched and can lead to genuine conversions, but its track record for growth beyond conversion is spotty at best, and
2) you can't trust well-executed programs to produce the spiritual growth that is lacking.

So how did Willow interpret the REVEAL data in terms of an action plan? Bill Hybels himself surmises:

We made a mistake. What we should have done when people crossed the line of faith and became Christians, we should have started telling people and teaching people that they have to take responsibility to become "self feeders." We should have gotten people, taught people, how to read their Bible between services, how to do the spiritual practices much more aggressively on their own.[2]

Now, insofar as he's talking about equipping and training, I think he's right on. We do need to teach people how to read their Bibles. (That Willow's REVEAL would call it a "breakthrough discovery" that reading the Bible is one of the top catalysts for spiritual growth seems a little odd!) Helping people to take responsibility for their faith and begin to live it out according to biblical wisdom in Christ is an important part of a church's discipleship of its people.

It's this other thing Hybels says that seems a little disconcerting. And we are hearing it more and more from leaders of other churches, not just the attractional types. It is this notion of self-feeding.

Again, if encouraging Christians to "self-feed" only means training and equipping them to practice spiritual disciplines, to take responsibility for their spiritual growth, then I think it is right. But if it is merely a reaction to the poor performance of the program system, sort of a "Well, they obviously don't need the church, so let's help them not need us," I think it can be one of those overcorrections that just leads to a whole new set of problems.

The last thing we need today, in a culture of lonely people practicing loneliness together, among people who from the beginning of time have been broken by pride and self-idolatry, is a concentrated focus on more solo Christianity. *Is more individualism really the answer?*

Somewhere between the poles of attachment to church programs and "self-feeding" lies the real stuff of covenant community. The church is the body of Christ, and we need it. We need community. We need the sustenance the community provides. And we need the shepherds who have been entrusted to feed us.

---

[2] Ibid.

Jesus Said, "Feed My Sheep"

In John 21:15, Jesus asks Peter a question. Basically, "Do you love me?"

Peter says yes.

And Jesus didn't say, "Then teach my sheep how to self-feed." No, he tells Peter, "Feed my lambs."

Jesus is referring to a shepherd's personal care for the flock, and specifically he is helping Peter see that his (Peter's) role must reflect the work of Christ himself. "If you love me," in other words, "you will do for others what I have done for you." And we do not see Jesus simply handing out resources and programs to his disciples, but sitting with them, walking with them, eating with them, praying with them, touching them and encouraging them and counseling them and correcting them. He does not hide behind his office door labeled "Messiah for Preaching and Vision." He is sweating and crying and sleeping in front of them. And he dies for them.

Jesus the pastor knows that the sheep need a shepherd (Matt. 9:36).

This doesn't mean an end to programmed provision. It doesn't mean we abandon our classes or our resource centers. What it does mean, though, is that we ought to put an end to the notion that The Program is the key to spiritual growth. It means we cannot install an event, and when we see it doesn't work, install another event and hope it succeeds.

Systems may aid the discipleship process, but discipleship is not a system. Discipleship is following Jesus. It requires help that is much more personal and relational.

The programmatic approach, and even the self-feeding approach, assumes that what people lack is a set of skills to address their felt needs for success or competence. But what any Christian enterprise ought to assume is that, beneath all our confusion and ignorance, what people really lack is a heart for God and neighbor. Underneath our felt needs is an entire industry of idols emerging from a foundation of sin and longing for glory. Only the gospel can get to that level and deal with it. This is why Jesus doesn't say, "teach my sheep," although he certainly wants us to teach. He says, "feed my sheep." Because he knows what we all really need first and foremost is the word of life that satisfies and sustains.

Isn't it odd that for so long we have begun with the idea that we must demonstrate how practical and applicable to everyday life Christianity is, yet so few people are actually being matured by the process that begins that way? I think it has something to do with the fact that we aren't beginning by addressing the real problem. We assume it is dysfunction or lack of success, when really it is sin. We need skills, sure. But we need grace first and most.

What good is it anyway to win people to the life of a church's programs if they aren't in love with Jesus? The attractional church too often holds up Jesus as more of a role model than the sovereign God, not so much as the Door as merely the doorman to success and happiness.

And so we have to give permission for someone to ask us the uncomfortable question at any given time: Are we trusting our programs, or are we trusting God?

I don't believe the right response to "the programs aren't working" is to conclude that the life of the church is not the place for Christians both new and "old" to be fed. I don't believe the right response to "our goods and services aren't having their desired effect" is to work on creating more independent Christians, trusting them to get it right somehow all by themselves. Whatever our programs, our churches' leaders need to take seriously the command of Christ—in as many ways as possible—to feed his sheep.

But this may require a radical reorienting not simply of programs or expectations but of the leader's aims. If we simply want more people or better people, a different set of programs and events might accomplish that. But if we want Christ-exalting, Christ-loving, Christ-following people, we have to get more personal and go deeper.

We have to get beyond simply trying to move warm bodies around through the systems and actually try moving the gospel into the system of those bodies. And that means figuring out the difference between managing people's activities and pastoring people's hearts.

Pastoring Hearts

In 2 Corinthians 3:1–3, Paul makes the important distinction between religious management and pastoral ministry:

> Are we beginning to commend ourselves again? Or do we need, as some do, letters of recommendation to you, or from you? You yourselves are our letter of recommendation, written on our hearts, to be known and read by all. And you show that you are a letter from Christ delivered by us, written not with ink but with the Spirit of the living God, not on tablets of stone but on tablets of human hearts.

The Corinthians are people he is trying to pastor. Yes, as an apostle, not as a local elder, but with the whole lot of 'em, Paul is experiencing normative pastoral ministry. Throughout both letters we have in our Bible from Paul to the Corinthian church, we see all the hallmarks of joyous, trying, exhilarating, agonizing, wonderful, terrible pastoral ministry. And what he is talking about in these three verses, as he connects himself (and the other leaders) to the Corinthians is utterly personal, utterly powerful, and utterly pastoral. The distinction he is making here between "letters written with ink on stone" versus "letters written by the Spirit on hearts" is how he differentiates his gospel ministry and missionary endeavors from the legal pontificating and persecution of his past.

And Paul is a guy who could simply write letters, giving out rebukes and commands, dispensing doctrine from afar. His travels could afford him a distance that would make such work very easy. But you don't get this sense in his letters. You see in fact how emotive he is, how heartfelt he is, how he in some sense wears his feelings on his sleeve—not in a whiny, pathetic way, but in a personal, honest, transparent way. He *feels* gospel ministry; he loves the people he is writing to. And he's not simply trying to push people around like game pieces on a board. He is, according to these three verses, seeking their hearts.

So what does this mean for those of us in ministry? What does pastoring hearts, as opposed to just pushing bodies around, mean? At least a few things:

Pastoring Hearts Means Resisting Pragmatism

Now, remember, pragmatism is not the same thing as being practical. There are lots of practical things in the Bible, and we would do well to teach them and help our churches embrace them. Faith without works is dead (James 2:17). Pragmatism, on the other hand, is the mind-set that says that whatever "works" can and should be used. If a particular method produces demonstrable and desirable results, the method is therefore authorized for use.

The problem with pragmatism, though, as we saw in chapter 3, is that it assumes that value is found only or primarily in something's apparent usefulness. In other words, if a particular practice does not appear to achieve regular results, it is deemed ineffective and useless. A pragmatic mind-set treats spiritual matters along the lines of mathematics.

I am reminded of Charles Finney's words on revival, where he says, "a revival is the result of the *right* use of the appropriate means."[3] In Finney's way of thinking, manufacturing revival is as simple as one plus one equaling two. You just need the right tools used in the right way. This is pragmatism.

We must remember that pastoral ministry, like Christianity itself, is not a matter of formulas but of faith.

It is so easy to think and minister in pragmatic ways, turning the work of Christian ministry into a kind of spiritual science or

---

[3] Charles G. Finney, *Lectures on Revivals of Religion*, 2nd ed. (New York: Leavitt, Lord, 1835), 12.

technology. If we just do *x*, then the result will be *y*. But Christian ministry is more messy than that. And as a ministry progresses, and perhaps growth is gained, the temptation becomes greater. Because when we're thinking at the thirty-thousand-foot level, it's easy to see people as little ants to manipulate. Or maybe we've taken the biblical sheep metaphor a bit *too* far, and we're looking at how best to *herd* the sheep instead of how best to feed them.

I believe pragmatism in the pastorate is killing the spiritual life of congregations, even congregations seeing an increase in attendance to Sunday worship. Despite the intricacy and efficiency of applied systems, many attenders of attractional churches get everything they want *except* pastoral care of their hearts. And more and more, this is appearing to be by design, as more and more leaders denigrate any layperson interested in being fed and cared for. They are called babies. They are told to grow up. They are told that the church is not for them. They are called Pharisees or "too religious." A sheep who wants to be fed is seen as someone in the way of the vision.

Look, it's not that we can't learn anything good from the titans of the pastoral industry. It is just that, more often than not, what is found in them that's good is not original, and what is found that's original is not good. Of course there are aspects of professionalism that make sense in our modern ministry contexts. But when all is said and done, we are not managers of spiritual enterprises: we are shepherds. And shepherds feed their sheep.

Paul says to the Corinthian Christians, "You are not letters written with ink on tablets of stone." What he was—and we are—speaking to is *hearts*.

Pastoring Hearts Means Being Present

Paul not only appeals to their hearts, but shows them his! "You yourselves are our letter of recommendation, written on our hearts," he says (2 Cor. 3:2).

How do you get people into your heart if you don't spend time with them? If you don't get among them, as Peter supposes pastors will be in 1 Peter 5:2?

What if Jesus saw us as we are so prone to see others? What if he regarded us as we regard others?

Picture *you* on your worst day. Maybe it's Monday morning. There you sit, a pitiful bump on a log. Sipping your coffee, feeling sorry for yourself, worn out and daydreaming of life as a UPS guy or whatever. Does Jesus look at you and mutter, "Ugh. This guy again?"

No, he feels compassion. He does not see us in the same way as we see the pop-in visitor approaching through the office door on Monday morning, or the troubled couple in need of counseling.

Jesus neither sulks nor sighs about us. He ministers to us willingly, eagerly. And there is power there to extend that ministry of reconciliation to others in the hardest times.

Paul says in chapter 1 of 2 Corinthians, "I want to visit with you again." He wants to be with them. In Galatians 4:20, "I wish I could be present with you now." To the Thessalonians, "[B]eing affectionately desirous of you, we were ready to share with you not only the gospel of God but also our own selves, because you had become very dear to us" (1 Thess. 2:8). To the Corinthians again, "Our heart is wide open" (2 Cor. 6.11).

We do not get the sense from Paul, not even from the original apostles who established the diaconate to take themselves away from table service (Acts 6), that personal presence with the sheep was optional. We see the elders charged with praying with people personally, teaching them personally, disciplining them personally, laying hands on them personally. Pastoral ministry is hands-on work.

Therefore, personal presence is so important. And I'd say you're not really a pastor if you're not present.

Pastoring Hearts Means Proclaiming the Gospel

This ain't some religious pep talk Paul is traveling the world to peddle. It's a "letter from Christ . . . written . . . with the Spirit of the living God" (2 Cor. 3:3). That is powerful stuff. That goes deeper than a set of life skills.

Only the gospel goes deep enough to effect real heart change. Everything else is just behavior modification.

This is certainly crucial in a pastor's preaching ministry. And as we preach the gospel, we will preach to both prodigals and older brothers. We will explain how the gospel is opposed to self-righteous religiosity. We will entreat both "brothers" to embrace Christ, the legalist as well as the hedonist. We won't give the impression that the gospel is just for those obvious sinners, the "lost" people, but for all people, including those who are in the pews every Sunday. But in order to reveal someone's functional ideology—what lies in their heart that drives them to act in legalistic ways or licentious ways—we have to employ the only tool adequate for that job, and that is the gospel of Jesus empowered by the Holy Spirit, not our dynamic preaching. No amount of rhetorical polish or captivating storytelling can do what the gospel does to get at hearts. Jonathan Edwards is one preacher known in history for his vivid imagery and profound effect on his hearers, yet Tim Keller says of Edwards,

> He understood that telling stories to tweak the emotions, is like putting dynamite on the face of the rock, blowing it up and shearing off the face but not really changing the life.
>
> [On] the other hand, if you bore down into it with the truth, and put dynamite in there, if you are able to preach Christ vividly, and you are able to preach the truth practically and you are able to preach it out of a changed life and heart in yourself (which obviously isn't the easiest thing by any means) then when there is an explosion, it really changes people's lives. I don't think we have the right end of the stick in general, either in the movement of the people who are working towards telling stories because they want to get people emotionally or working towards giving people the truth because they want to be sure that people are doctrinally sound.[4]

---

[4] Tim Keller, "Gospel-Centered Ministry," *The Spurgeon Fellowship Journal* (Spring 2008), 4, http://issuu .com/gospeldelta/docs/tim-keller-gospel-centered-ministry.

Only the gospel gets down into the heart. So in our counseling, in our visits, in our staff devotionals and instructional time, we must administer Christ, not simply advice.

Pastoring Hearts Means Seeking Souls, Not Stats

Paul says of the Corinthians, "you show that you are a letter from Christ delivered by us" (2 Cor. 3:3). Therein lies the difference between disciple-producing and decision-producing.

The way we are typically programmed to measure the success of our ministries sets us up for hollow victory and desperate failure. But this is not to say we should never do any measuring. It is only to say that what we measure and how we measure shows where our confidence lies.

For instance, not all attendance increases are created equal. Joel Osteen boasts the largest church in North America, but it is not likely that the majority of these attendees are feeding on the gospel, because Osteen does not preach it as "of first importance." For that matter, the Mormons, whom Osteen considers fellow Christians,[5] are a movement growing in numbers and influence. There are many false religions with many adherents around the world. Clearly, accumulating numbers cannot be our primary measure of success.

But in the attractional church, growth in numbers is often seen not just as a measure of success but as a justification for any methodology used to get them. Numbers become not just a metric to track growth but a badge of honor and a demand for validation. It is not uncommon to see the leaders of attractional churches tallying each week in public venues the number of "decisions" that were made. (This is at least a more honest label than "salvations," since it would seem presumptuous to declare the number of souls changed by virtue of the number of feet down an aisle or names on a card.) Where any church sees the fruit of gospel preaching, both

---

[5] Paul Stanley, "Joel Osteen: Mormon Romney Is a Christian; Obama Is Too," *Christian Post* online (April 25, 2012), http://www.christianpost.com/news/joel-osteen-mormon-romney-is-christian-obama-is-too-73826/.

in professions of faith and in the baptisms by which the professions are announced, we all ought to rejoice with those who rejoice. But we also ought to caution those who publicly tally to check their own motives and observe their disciples' fruit. Biblical credibility is not found in big stats.

Apparently this phenomenon is not new, as Spurgeon once responded to it himself:

> Do not, therefore, consider that soul-winning is or can be secured by the multiplication of baptisms and the swelling of the size of your church. What mean these dispatches from the battlefield? "Last night fourteen souls were under conviction, fifteen were justified, and eight received full sanctification." I am weary of this public bragging, this counting of unhatched chickens, this exhibition of doubtful spoils. Lay aside such numberings of the people, such idle pretense of certifying in half a minute that which will need the testing of a lifetime.[6]

The attractional defenders of such number-crunching will say that numbers matter because every number is a person and every person matters. Absolutely right. But every person is a soul, and when in our zeal we pronounce the state of a soul that has not been invested in over time and cared for, we do no one's soul any favors.

Another thing we often hear as a church growth truism is that "healthy things grow." And as I said before, yes, they often do. But not always.

Pastoral ministry is about souls, not stats. If your number of souls grows, fantastic. To God be the glory. Let's just remember that we are responsible mainly for the care of the souls, not the accumulation of them.

In the end, this is good news. It is good news because it means God's approval of us is not based on our ability to produce statistics. We are not called to be successful but faithful. We may plant, we may water, but it is God who gives the growth (1 Cor. 3:6).

---

[6] Charles Spurgeon, *The Soulwinner* (New Kensington, PA: Whitaker, 1995), 13.

When we pastors cling to the gospel ourselves, it will shape us, giving us the mind and heart of Christ for our people. As Christ shepherds our hearts, let us shepherd the hearts of our people, with deep love and spiritual affection seeking their good above our own comfort. And in the end, they may be our boast (2 Cor. 1:14).

8

A Way Forward

Well, either you've made it this far, or you just happened to open the book to this page randomly—perhaps in the store. If this is the first page you've read, please go back and start at the beginning, you cheater! If you have read all the pages before this one, first, Thank You! I imagine you found some of the material up to this point either challenging or redundant, or perhaps both. That is by design. I have wanted to challenge your assumptions and convictions. And I've wanted to repeat myself on a number of important issues in service of that challenge. Like I said in chapter 1, I did intend to pester you.

But even if you're not like me in how you do church, I'll bet you're like me and a whole lot of other people in that, when you hear someone criticizing something long enough, eventually you want to know what answers they have. It's very easy to complain. Complaints are a dime a dozen. It's easy to sit back and point out flaws and faults. It's a special critic, though, who doesn't just find problems but does so first from love and secondly with solutions in mind. By now, you know what this book is against. But what is it *for*?

I trust you've been able to discern the answer to that question along the way, as I've offered some alternatives bit by bit to the attractional approaches I've critiqued. The central idea of the church should be the gospel. That is my main thesis. How that central idea works out practically has been hinted at in the previous chapters, but in this chapter I hope to spell it out further.

I do want to tell you, though, that if you are looking for a formula or system or program as the offered antidote to the problematic formulas, systems, and programs I've been criticizing, you will be further disappointed. There are certainly things to do, and I will suggest several. But in the end, when I say the central idea of the church should be the gospel, I am presupposing that it is God who determines who gets success and who doesn't. And if you'll review that last sentence again, you may be struck that I am suggesting that success isn't a foregone conclusion in church ministry. It may be that God is calling us to die in order to fertilize the ground for the next guy's success. And in the paradigm of the gospel's sufficiency in all of life for all of eternity, "failing" in order to help the next guy succeed is a great work.

So what is the way forward for the church interested in diverging from the attractional trajectory? What are some initial shifts that should take place?

Measuring the Right Things

Jesus tells a story about talents that is instructive:

> For it will be like a man going on a journey, who called his servants and entrusted to them his property. To one he gave five talents, to another two, to another one, to each according to his ability. Then he went away. He who had received the five talents went at once and traded with them, and he made five talents more. So also he who had the two talents made two talents more. But he who had received the one talent went and dug in the ground and hid his master's money. Now after a long time the master of those servants came and settled accounts with them. And he who had received the five talents came forward, bringing five talents more, saying, "Master, you

delivered to me five talents; here I have made five talents more."
His master said to him, "Well done, good and faithful servant.
You have been faithful over a little; I will set you over much.
Enter into the joy of your master." And he also who had the
two talents came forward, saying, "Master, you delivered to me
two talents; here I have made two talents more." His master said
to him, "Well done, good and faithful servant. You have been
faithful over a little; I will set you over much. Enter into the joy
of your master." He also who had received the one talent came
forward, saying, "Master, I knew you to be a hard man, reap-
ing where you did not sow, and gathering where you scattered
no seed, so I was afraid, and I went and hid your talent in the
ground. Here you have what is yours." But his master answered
him, "You wicked and slothful servant! You knew that I reap
where I have not sown and gather where I scattered no seed?
Then you ought to have invested my money with the bankers,
and at my coming I should have received what was my own
with interest." (Matt. 25:14–27)

We can learn a few points of application from this parable, and
one of them is that God doesn't give the same amount of gifts and
resources to everyone. Some are entrusted with a little, some are entrusted with a lot. But all who receive from the Lord are entrusted
with what they receive. So we also learn from this parable that it
doesn't so much matter how much you have, but rather what you
do with it. Jesus drives the point home this way in Luke 16:10:
"One who is faithful in a very little is also faithful in much, and one
who is dishonest in a very little is also dishonest in much."

Numbers don't account for everything. In some cases, they don't
account for anything. You can be a poor steward with a lot or you
can be a faithful steward with a little. What God will require of us
is not ministry quantity but ministry quality.

But we have to be careful with measuring quality, too.

The environmental experience of some attractional churches
often boils down to a series of questions like these:

- Does the worship service feel exciting and relevant to you?
- Do you enjoy the music?
- Is the message inspiring?
- Are you made to feel special when you're there?
- Do your kids have a good time in the children's ministry?

But none of these questions are particularly spiritual. None of these means of measurement help us gauge the actual value of a church experience, according to the Bible. They could just as easily apply to a visit to Disney World. They are more reminiscent of a customer-satisfaction survey. So these sorts of questions work fine in an attractional church where consumerism and pragmatism are the functional ideologies, but in a church centered on the gospel, things like inspiration and good feelings are seen as byproducts of the experiences, not the aim of the experiences.

So we look to measure other things first. Perhaps a more relevant list of questions might look like this:

- Are those being baptized continuing to walk in the faith a year later? Two years? Three years?
- How many of our people are being trained to personally disciple others?
- What percentage of our weekend attendees are engaged in community groups? Evangelism? Community service?
- How many of our people could articulate the biblical gospel?
- What is the reputation of our church in the community?
- As our people graduate to higher levels in our training programs, do they demonstrate a growing understanding of theology and a growing walk with Christ?

These things are harder to measure, certainly, but they tell us more than mere numbers and experiential feelings, and they are therefore more valuable kinds of measurements.

This is the difference between merely counting numbers and actually measuring real growth. It is the difference between amassing a crowd and making disciples. The former motivations are what keep us constantly innovating, trying to stay ahead of the cultural winds (even though the church nearly always finds itself following them):

This is why we are such suckers for the latest ministry expert, who has always grown a church of at least 5000 from scratch, and who has a guaranteed method for growing your church to be like his. Every five or ten years, a new wave comes through. It might be the seeker-service model, or the purpose-driven model, or the missional-cultural-engagement model, or whatever the next thing will be. All of these methodologies have good things going for them, but all of them are equally beside the point—because our goal is not to grow churches, but to make disciples.[1]

The attractional church's emphasis on decisions comes closest to this area of actual health, but a gospel-centered church will probe deeper, seeking to grow what is showing some promise rather than declaring victory by simply counting raised hands.

What is emphasized and valued in a church's media correlates to what that church is measuring as success. The attractional church, which places a huge emphasis on numbers, size, and raw data, highly prizes statistics. The gospel-centered church highly prizes stories. Rather than prizing bigness, it prizes relationality. Big or small, it is clear that the emphasis is not on events or experiences but on engaging people with the biblical story of redemption and helping people engage each other with the ongoing story of redemption in their daily lives.

The attractional church needs to challenge itself on whether some of its expressed values actually stifle the redemptive quality of the gospel's work on the people it is trying to reach. Consider this reflection from the *Leadership Journal* blog:

Last year I met with a team of leaders from my church. Our task: to rethink and rearticulate the guiding values of our

---

[1] Colin Marshall and Tony Payne, *The Trellis and the Vine: The Ministry Mind-Shift That Changes Everything* (Kingsford, NSW, Australia: Matthias Media: 2009), 151.

congregation. The work was relatively easy. Upon investigation we determined that most of our core values hadn't shifted. We still believed in the centrality of relationships to ministry, our bent toward creativity, and the importance of participation. But then we came to "excellence."

For years our church has listed "excellence" as one of its core values. Support for this word, if not the idea behind it, has been slipping for years. A growing number of leaders are uncomfortable with excellence for a number of reasons. Perhaps the most common objection is that it's a more subtle way of saying we are perfectionists. Others object that the word is off-putting to people in the church that cannot achieve "excellence." It's exclusionary.

Defenders of the term say it has nothing to do with perfectionism or elitism, but a desire to "do our very best for God." And one person's very best may differ significantly from another's, but both are upholding the value of excellence. In the end the decision was made to change the articulation of the value and drop the word "excellence." But what word should we use?

Daniel Schantz . . . wrote an insightful, dare I say excellent, article about the increasing discomfort with the notion of excellence in the church. . . . Here is a brief excerpt:

> The term excellence is often spoken by church leaders in condescending tones, as if to say, "Others may be content with being average slobs, but not us. We must have only the best." This can be a slap in the face to members who don't have the capacity or means to be excellent— the "good," the "fair," the "poor."
>
> Can only good-looking, gifted singers serve on the worship team? Must church buildings resemble palaces in order to be useful? Do all preachers have to be Madison Avenue models, professional comedians, celebrities, best-selling authors, and able to speak five languages? The gospel was targeted to the poor, not just to the exceptional.

Schantz's article reads like a transcript from one of our church leadership meetings. He captures the arguments surrounding the term "excellence" perfectly. But the question remains—is there a positive alternative? What word should replace excellence in our ecclesiastical lexicon? Or, are you a true believer in excellence who is willing to fight the slippery slope of mediocrity?[2]

Commenters on the blog offered some good suggestions—faithfulness, authenticity, etc. I think much core-value terminology has the tendency to lapse into meaningless jargon—*buzzwordism*, if you will. Ponder the uselessness of the word "authenticity" in church marketing. Do most congregations even know what their church's "core values" are? I think of such things like I do mission and vision statements. They don't hurt, but really, are they consciously driving the people of the church?

But the biggest problem with a church's core values being reduced to things like "creativity" and "innovation" and "excellence" is how biblically deficient such prioritizing is. Creativity and innovation and excellence are all good things; they are all important things that can bring God glory. But if you were to search out the Bible's suggestions for a church's "core values," would that short list match most churches' short lists?

None of our churches want to present lousy stuff to our people and to our communities. No one's intentionally trying to make bad music or preach bad sermons. But when we run the other way, pursuing the notion of excellence like an idol, are we communicating something that actually discourages real people with real problems from risking embarrassment or judgment by telling their story of un-excellence? If we make excellence a "core value," are we inadvertently saying to people who struggle and fail that we don't value *them*?

---

[2] "An Alternative to 'Excellence'," Leadership Journal Parse blog (January 2, 2008), http://www.christianity today.com/parse/2008/january/alternative-to-excellence.html.

162 The Prodigal Church

In our striving for authenticity, are we coming across, to those who want something deeper than a well-produced experience, as inauthentic?

We might need to start learning to measure the right things.

Part of moving forward and away from the functional ideologies of the attractional church is also abandoning ourselves to the sovereign mercy of the Spirit, who cannot be measured or leveraged or synergized or *whatever*. Part of the attractional church's fundamental deficiency is a fear of ceding control.

You Can't Program Discipleship (Because Christianity Is Supernatural)

How often we forget this! Christianity is supernatural. It comes from God, works by God, and looks to God.

We are not dealing with a life system, a religious code, a set of tips or instructions for more successful living or modified behavior. Christianity is about the raising of the dead.

Would anyone, after receiving the latest gobbledygook from Tony Robbins or Oprah Winfrey, write a song like this?

> Long my imprisoned spirit lay,
> fast bound in sin and nature's night;
> thine eye diffused a quickening ray;
> I woke, the dungeon flamed with light;
> my chains fell off, my heart was free,
> I rose, went forth, and followed thee.[3]

We are not saved, as Donald Whitney says, by *sola boot strappa*. We are saved by grace alone, received through faith alone. And this is not the result of our works, lest any of us should boast. It comes from the Lord. Ever and always.

The message of the gospel is an announcement about what God has done in Christ, and when it goes forth in power it is because

---

[3] Charles Wesley, "And Can It Be That I Should Gain?" (1738).

God has done it. The gospel is not made more powerful by a dynamic preacher or a rockin' band; those things might adorn the gospel in an excellent way, but the gospel cannot be improved. The message of Christ's sinless life, sacrificial death, and glorious resurrection is capital-S Spiritual power all unto itself. Mark Dever writes,

> Conversion certainly includes our own actions. We must make a sincere commitment. We must make a self-conscious decision. Even so, conversion—real conversion—is more than that. Scripture is clear in teaching that we are not all journeying toward God—some having found Him, others still seeking. Instead, Scripture presents us as needing to have our hearts replaced, our minds transformed, our spirits given life. We can do none of this for ourselves. The change each human needs, regardless of how we may outwardly appear, is so radical, so near our roots, that only God can bring it about. We need God to convert us.
>
> I fear that one of the results of misunderstanding the Bible's teaching on conversion may well be that evangelical churches are full of people who have made sincere commitments at some point in their lives but who have not experienced the radical change that the Bible calls conversion.[4]

Comparatively speaking, it is much easier to gather up "decisions." But the work of heart change we are actually supposed to be after comes only from God's Spirit. The gospel that saved us ought to be a reminder itself that, for all the earthiness, for all the natural means, for all the restoration of the creation that God is doing, Christianity is sourced in God himself in heaven above. It is supernatural.

One of our church's most vivid examples of the supernaturality of Christianity is my friend Steven. Steven showed up in our church one Sunday morning three years ago. I don't always get to meet visitors on their first time, but I did get to meet Steven on his

4 Mark Dever, *Nine Marks of a Healthy Church* (Wheaton, IL: Crossway, 2004), 113.

first morning in our church, and I'm glad I did, because it was his first time in any church anywhere in forty-four years.

Steven had left the Roman Catholic church of his upbringing when he was eighteen and never looked back. Now at sixty-two years of age, his heart had been longing for spiritual truth. The Lord was wanting to bring him to himself. But I can't tell you Steven's story without telling you about another man, named Bruce.

Bruce is a former Jehovah's Witness. He began coming to our church four years ago. He didn't believe then and doesn't believe now (at least, as of this writing) the biblical truths of evangelical Christianity. His points of contention continue to be the doctrines of the Trinity and the deity of Christ, but he also disputes salvation by grace alone. Bruce maintains a few of the peculiar doctrines of the Jehovah's Witnesses, but in general, he says that everything is on the table. He comes to our church not because he believes everything we teach but because he likes to hear teaching from the Bible and he especially likes being with our people, who are exceedingly gracious and sweet and hospitable.

One day Steve was at Bruce's place doing some work on his property. Steve told Bruce he had been experiencing a pull back to some kind of spirituality. Steve's brother is a believer in Christ and had been telling him he ought to start going to church again. When Steve said this to Bruce, Bruce said, "Well, you ought to come with me some Sunday to Middletown." So Steve did, and now we're caught back up to the beginning of the story.

Two years ago, Steve made a profession of faith in Jesus Christ, and I baptized him in Lake St. Catherine one August afternoon. In the last three years he has not missed a single Sunday of gathered worship. He shows up early to our weekly men's discipleship group, and he is a voracious reader of the Bible and an eager and curious student of the things of God. He is growing by leaps and bounds and is actively engaged in seeking to evangelize his family and friends.

Now, I have to tell you: our church could not have even begun to come up with the strategy that God used to get Steven saved. We *wouldn't* have come up with the idea in the first place. I could not have sat down with the elders one evening at our meeting and said, "You know who's an untapped resource for bringing people into our church? The Jehovah's Witnesses!" I would've gotten fired for even suggesting it!

And yet here Steve is, a testimony to the Holy Spirit's power and working. Let us never forget that Christianity is supernatural. You cannot program salvation.

The gospel message itself is supernatural. The life we have, Paul says, is not from "the letter" but from "the Spirit" (2 Cor. 3:6). God is at work in the gospel. It comes from him, it is empowered by him, and it works through him.

Preaching is itself a supernatural act. And you will preach the gospel in different ways in different situations. But regardless of the situation or context, you will want to make sure the central idea in your ministry is the gospel of Jesus Christ. Because only the gospel is power (Rom. 1:16; 1 Cor. 1:18; Eph. 3:7; 1 Thess. 1:5).

The gospel does the work. If you want your people to be trained in righteousness, to be good repenters and in pursuit of holiness, Titus 2:11 says it is grace that does that. If you want your church to become more Christlike, in suffering and out, 2 Corinthians 3:18 says it's by beholding Jesus that they are transformed. If you want them to become imitators of Christ, disciples in the kingdom, even in the midst of suffering, 1 Thessalonians 1:6 says this happens by receiving the Word in the midst of affliction.

The Holy Spirit working through the good news is the only power we've got!

Now, we come to the table of vision with our big ideas and our systems in hand. But the frustrating thing about the Holy Spirit is that you cannot control him. We once had a couple attending our church, where the husband was a believer and his wife was not.

He had prayed for years for her conversion. We had prayed for this together. Many in our church prayed that, by regular exposure to the grace of God in our church, she would come to know the Lord.

One day this couple had to move away. A few months later, I got an excited message from my friend. He said, "Good news! My wife has come to the Lord!"

Of course, I responded along the lines of, "That's fantastic! Congratulations!" But inside, I was grumbling a little. "Why not here, Lord?" I mean, what did that church have that we didn't have? She certainly heard the gospel here. She certainly was welcomed and loved here.

The frustrating thing is that we cannot control the Holy Spirit.

I think of another married couple, an elderly couple this time, each of whom was on their deathbed. She was in a nursing home dying of cancer. He was in a hospital dying of emphysema. I visited both husband and wife, spoke tenderly and clearly to them both, sharing the gospel with both of them. She accepted Christ. He did not. What was the difference? Why did one profess faith and the other did not?

The Holy Spirit reminds his churches, "I'm not a formula. The wind blows where it wishes, and you hear its sound, but you do not know where it comes from or where it goes. So it is with everyone who is born of the Spirit."

The Spirit doesn't wear the church's wristwatch. You cannot control him.

The message, the methods, the means, all have to come from God, or we're completely sunk. This means at the very minimum that our ministry, like our Christian life in general, ought to be saturated in prayer.

Do you know why we don't pray more? It's because we think we are sufficient in ourselves (2 Cor. 3:5). We don't pray more because we don't feel helpless more. That's what prayer is, essentially: acknowledged helplessness.

The Spirit has done such powerful things for our church that we could never have done, even if we had tried! Even if we'd had a plan, a strategy, a well-ordered system. But we do not worship the Father, the Son, and The Holy Ingenuity.

The men of God in the Scriptures walked in the power of the Spirit, because they knew they needed the Lord God to live. They had nothing of their own to offer, apart from God. The best we can muster up is symbolic. But when the Lord moves through us, he moves in great power to transform.

Indeed, we can do nothing apart from the Holy Spirit. You could not get up this morning apart from the Holy Spirit. You cannot take your next breath apart from the Holy Spirit. And if your next breath is your last breath, you could not get into the everlasting rest of Christ's glory apart from the Holy Spirit. It is "in him," Paul says to the men of the Areopagus, that "we live and move and have our being" (Acts 17:28). This means that apart from him, we do not live, we do not move, we do not *be*.

When some of John the Baptist's disciples are arguing with some Jews about purification in John 3, the Baptist himself says, "A person cannot receive *even one thing* unless it is given him from heaven" (v. 27). Paul says to the church at Colossae, "For this I toil, struggling with all *his energy* that he powerfully works within me" (Col. 1:29).

This ought to make us despair of ourselves and trust unreservedly in God. And the result is: we will have a boldness we wouldn't have had if Christianity were simply about spiritual mathematics. When the Spirit who is God is active and real and leading us into all truth, we can have real confidence. If I am united to Christ, I am as secure as Christ is. The freedom that comes from this reality is extraordinarily empowering.

Everything good and valuable must come from the Spirit's sovereign working, not from our ministerial machinations.

Yes, the frustrating thing about the Holy Spirit is that you cannot control him.

And the wonderful thing about the Holy Spirit is that you cannot control him! There is no heart too hard, no soul too cold, no situation so bleak, no spirit too imprisoned, no life too dead for the third person of the Trinity. The Holy Spirit is still roaming the earth, seeking whom he may revive. And wherever the gospel is going forth, the Spirit is doing whatever God pleases.

Christian ministry is supernatural. And the gospel-centered church knows that moving people along the path of discipleship may entail measuring different things, promoting different things, and preaching different things. It doesn't negate the use of programs or systems; it just doesn't put its trust in them.

In the attractional world, after all, it's still possible that the pragmatic means of programming actually serves to cultivate the *opposite* of what's intended. Those making decisions may be won not to Christ the Lord but to Christ the Example. They may be won not to the church but to an event. They may be converted not to Christian community but to religious activity. You can't program discipleship.

Sometimes we expect programs to meet needs that our people don't even feel. Sometimes we expect the existence of the programs themselves to stir desire for the programs. One of the areas in which this is most prominent is in the desire to foster a deeper experience of "community." Many churches certainly think that way when it comes to moving people further along, from attending a weekend experience and into life-on-life relationships with the people of the church. But how we preach might be working against all the appeals we make for small group participation.

Community Begins on Sunday Morning

If you're like most church leaders, you have likely expected your small groups program to nurture a sense of community in your church and the increase of relational intimacy among your people. Perhaps you use these groups as a springboard to community service and evangelistic hospitality as well. And if you're like most leaders, you have probably discovered that building a successful small groups program has proven more difficult than expected. Only recently are some national leaders admitting that very few churches are doing small groups well, and some are even suggesting that the prevailing blueprints for community don't work at all.

Whether it's the blueprints or the way they're carried out, more and more churches are struggling to make community "happen," and this great need continues to be met with an ever-increasing supply of books, kits, systems, and conferences, all designed to ignite small group success.

If it's not the formula we're after, it's the right leader. Peruse any of the major ministry job lists, and you will see the growing proliferation of ads for discipleship and spiritual formation pastors, nearly all of them requesting that applicants demonstrate previous experience in building successful small group programs. As I talk to more and more pastors concerned about the quality of community in their congregations, I am hearing more and more the insistence that, if you don't have a vibrant small groups program, all you need is the right leader to make it happen.

The evangelical church's search for the magic bullet is insatiable. But is the great hope for small groups a plan or its planner? Many church leaders face the hard truth too late in the game: if you don't have a congregation that *cares* about small groups, it doesn't matter what kind of program or leader you throw at the need; your congregation isn't suddenly going to care about small groups.

Pastors, the nurturing of your congregation's desire for experiential community begins with you. It begins with your shepherding of the weekly gathering. *Your weekend service has a direct effect on how your congregation thinks and acts.* It's supposed to, right? You trust that all the time and energy and preparation poured into the worship service is impacting lives and is being used by God to mature your congregation.

So do the math. If, despite the different programs and leaders you've thrown at the small groups gap in your church, you still can't get people interested in small groups, it might be time to rethink the message your weekend gathering is sending and the sort of impact it is having.

The truth is that your weekly teaching can radically transform the quality of community in your church and lead directly to the success of your small groups programs.

The logic is simple but somehow evasive for so many pastors. If week in and week out you are feeding your congregation a steady diet of self-help and personal improvement, of individual application for one's walk with Jesus as their "personal" Lord and Savior, you may not exactly be stirring the desire in them to be connected to other believers. If your preaching is consistently of the "How to Win at Work" or "How to Be Your Best You" variety, you may be feeding and coddling the individualism of the average churchgoer and reinforcing the values of the consumerist culture he must live and work in every day.

This does not mean, of course, that the Bible says nothing about individual discipleship or our personal lives, whether lived at work or home or play, only that it says much more about Christians living their lives as part of the body of Christ. The biblical blueprint for discipleship is community, so any discipleship training tips you supply from the pulpit or stage should be reframed to the context of the church community. Make it abundantly clear that discipleship to Jesus is more about walking alongside other disciples than it is about improving one's own stride.

This change in course could be as radical as teaching through the book of Acts or borrowing from Dietrich Bonhoeffer's classic book *Life Together*,[5] or it can be as simple as changing the applicational focus of your message from what individuals can do to what your church can do together. For example, you can replace

---

[5] Dietrich Bonhoeffer, *Life Together* (New York: HarperOne, 2009)

repeated calls to your congregation to be kind to their unchurched neighbors with an announcement about an ongoing neighborhood effort your church designs for groups to serve in together, such as volunteering with Habitat for Humanity, supplying a food pantry, or conducting block parties.

You may also stir a greater desire for community by switching out pop culture references and generic illustrations for stories from actual people in the life of your church. I remember the evening our small group in a previous church was awed into silence, a rare occasion for us! It was the result of hearing these words from a visitor: "I became a Christian a few months ago. If I go back home, they will kill me."

After a pregnant pause, our Iranian immigrant friend added, "But it's okay."

We were floored. *This* was real faith. This was the amazing grace of the gospel, lived out by a very brave woman. And she was sitting with fellow Christians in a Nashville café, drinking coffee and talking about life. This is something none of us would have heard up close if not for the powerful intimacy of community.

These are the kinds of stories we should be sharing in our teaching. A great way to stir your people toward craving community is by highlighting some of the cherished moments occurring in the groups that already exist. Talk about their service projects, talk about their effectual prayers, talk about their cooperation. If you use video elements in your worship service, have your team conduct interviews with people who have been impacted by their time in small groups.

These efforts at providing real-life glimpses into community in action can be incredibly inspiring. Previously unmotivated churchgoers may be struck by a story or inspired by a personal testimony to say to themselves, "I want that too." This is a great way of putting a face on your call for community, a relatable way of saying, "This works."

And then, of course, you know by now that I have to "go there."

One reason our people lack a desire for community is that we have not preached the whole counsel of Scripture as it relates to the primary message with which we are charged: the gospel of Jesus Christ.

My thesis is this: small group programs don't succeed apart from a consistent, determined gospel-driven nurturing of the value of community in the weekend worship service. For many preachers, contemplating the implications of this redirect can cause a crisis of teaching conscience. But God has promised that his word will not return void. If we will commit to preaching the truth that embracing Jesus Christ means dying to ourselves and repenting of our self-centeredness, he will produce the fruit of discipleship in community within our churches.

Remember that the fall didn't place enmity only between man and God; it also placed enmity between man and woman. The fall caused division between me and God and division between me and my neighbor. So the gospel isn't just about my being reconciled to God, but also about my being reconciled to you.

Good, robust gospel preaching will routinely reinforce that Jesus doesn't just connect us to God; he connects us to each other. In his High Priestly Prayer, just before his death, Jesus prayed that the community of his followers would be one, and he died and rose to make it so.

What an incredible and powerful truth! See how enormous and satisfying the gospel is? Let's put Jesus at the center of our preaching and the fullness of his reconciliation at the forefront of our calls to follow him.

Finally, we have to trust the Spirit to put desires where they currently are not. We cannot trust ourselves. So if at first we see no visible results, we walk by faith in God's Word, setting aside our hope in advertising, and adopting a posture of patience and trust.

Reject the tyranny of results. There is no quick fix. Any of these efforts implemented just a few weeks before your next small groups semester will look like what they are: advertisements for the program.

Instead, implement these changes and others over the long haul. It takes a lot of effort and patience and endurance to transform a congregational culture. Think long term. As you are motivating, realize you are cultivating, and know that cultivation is a long process. Take the time to plant seeds for relational intimacy in the hearts of your congregants, and be sensitive to the Spirit as you nurture their growth over time. And pray, pray, pray.

Preach hard on the cost of discipleship, on the call to community, and adhere to that hard preaching in (to borrow from Eugene Peterson) "a long obedience in the same direction."

If we want to cultivate disciples, if we want to alter the DNA of our churches to better reflect the reconciliation of the gospel, the investment will be worth it.

Become Self-Critical

So much of the way forward involves putting everything on the table for renegotiation. Not the Bible, of course. Not the basic tenets of Christian orthodoxy. But our methods and our assumptions about "how it works."

Every church needs people authorized by those with the most authority to say, "This is a bad idea." About anything. Maybe one of those people is the one who handed you this book. Don't get mad at him. Consider what he has to say. Prove him wrong, if you must. But don't quiet the questions before they can be asked.

Too many folks in the attractional church have shut off all openness to criticism. I know the main reasons why. Criticism stinks. It's often hurtful and hateful. It's too often ignorant and unrelational.

But we can learn from (some of) our critics. If we will have the humility in ourselves and the confidence in Christ to listen to them. To weigh their thoughts. To resist the knee-jerk reactions of writing them off as jealous haters or bitter legalists.

If you're still reading this book, I assume you are halfway there with me. Meaning, I assume you are open to considering this critique and weighing the proposed way forward. Maybe you're reading out of pride, because I dared you at the beginning. Maybe you plan to get your money back, but just want to be honest about having read the whole thing. In any event, I urge you to listen to the critical voices that love you. Begin by inviting trusted people on your team or in your accountability circles to speak the truth to you. Authorize them to question you. Give permission for someone with biblical maturity and your best interest in mind to say, about anything, "This is a bad idea."

You don't have to be an attractional guy to be allergic to dissent. I don't like criticism either, even if it's constructive, and especially when it's valid. My defenses go up and my excuses come out. Deep down, I want the yes men. But one of the best things I've done for my personal walk with Christ and for the health of my church is have people around me in positions of leadership and authority who are able to speak truth into my life. They can ask tough questions. They can call me out. They can critique the "vision." They can play devil's advocate. Because I know, (1) they love me and our church, and (2) I'm not infallible.

Sometimes I'm just plain stupid. And so my way forward includes not assuming that every good idea I have is actually good.

Questions to Ask on the Way Forward

As I've said, some of the unhelpful elements in our worship services could be eliminated if only those in the planning stages were allowed to ask better questions, which is to say, more "first principle," self-reflective questions. I have some suggestions.

Of course, these aren't the only questions worth asking, but perhaps they'll provide some good guardrails for those involved in planning worship gatherings, from sermon prep to music selection to sacraments to announcements and all the other nuts and bolts of a service. Here is a rough outline of some good lines of inquiry:

1. Is there support for this service element in the Scriptures?
Even if you're not a regulative principle church, this is a non-negotiable.

2. Is this element comprehensible to outsiders?
Total understanding of every element is not possible, of course, and spiritual acceptance isn't possible for those outside the faith, but unbelievers and other visitors should be able to discern *what* you're doing, even if they don't know why you're doing it.

3. Is this element edifying to believers?
Not simply, is this entertaining or amusing, or will this attract attention, or provoke? But, is this edifying? Is it conducive to the building up of the saints in Christ and in God's love? Does it directly serve that purpose? Or is it here just to entertain?

4. Is this element offensive, alienating, or marginalizing to any section or subsection of the church body?
People scoff when they hear the complaints about music being too loud, but so often this is a legitimate concern for older folks. People may disregard music or sermons that are boring or boringly presented, but so often this is a legitimate concern for younger folks. You obviously can't please everyone, but our service elements should not be approached insensitively or with disregard for the reality of the body—all the members of it. Sometimes in our churches we make accommodations for certain groups knowing full well that those accommodations will alienate others, and we end up making some dear people feel like second-class citizens in the church. It is important that we not challenge the stylistic idolatries of one demographic by employing the stylistic idolatries of another. What serves? What ministers? What appropriately allows for participation in the service across the body of Christ? On that note:

5. Does this element exalt God, or man?

Apply as needed to everything from sermon points to special music. It's not about denigrating man, or not recognizing people for various achievements and the like. It is just a good question to ask as it pertains to the focus of a worship service.

6. Does this element adorn the gospel?

Is this element in service of the gospel or of some other message or focus? Or, alternately, does this element in the worship service magnify Jesus, or ourselves?

The point, of course, is not that we create a culture of cynicism or permit critical spirits to run loose in our leadership ranks or in the discipleship culture of the church in general. The point is that we allow good, penetrating questions that help us be appropriately self-critical and self-correcting. We need the guardrails of good theology and thoughtful application. I know it stinks when enthusiasm for a particular idea or initiative gets tempered by a "yes, but," but the church does not exist to facilitate all our good ideas. Good intentions and strong giftedness do not baptize unbiblical methods.

The way forward, away from the thoughtless license of the attractional church, begins with handing out swords to your people and charging them with gutting the idols of consumerism and pragmatism. It begins with seeking the magnification of Christ above and beyond any showmanship we think might serve that end.

He must increase; we must decrease.

9

The Prodigal Church
Comes Home

"Cheap grace is the deadly enemy of our Church. We are fighting to-day for costly grace."[1]

Thus begins the important book *The Cost of Discipleship*, in which German Lutheran pastor Dietrich Bonhoeffer discusses the weight and responsibility of following Jesus. (Bonhoeffer would know a little something about "cost," as he was executed by the Third Reich for conspiring against Adolf Hitler.) What Bonhoeffer means by "cheap grace" is the kind of sentimental notion of God's approval that allows professing believers to demonstrate no serious change in their lives. God becomes an add-on. Jesus is the spiritual guru we most admire. We "come to Jesus" for the benefit of his promise of eternal life—the ticket to heaven—but when it comes to taking up our crosses, you know, *we'd rather not*.

The church that deals in cheap grace, Bonhoeffer goes on to say, is only dealing with grace as a concept and not with real grace at all. It has traded in the living God for some kind of abstraction, an idea. Consequently, with true grace not in play, there is no real forgiveness of sins taking place. "In such a Church," he writes, "the

---

[1] Dietrich Bonhoeffer, *The Cost of Discipleship* (New York: Touchstone, 1995), 41.

world finds a cheap covering for its sins; no contrition is required, still less any real desire to be delivered from sin."[2]

That is a key point for our examination of the attractional paradigm and the re-centering on the gospel. People in a church that is centered on meeting felt needs or satisfying stylistic preferences or reflecting the culture are not frequently compelled to despair of themselves and find refuge in the grace of God in Christ. They are instead frequently compelled to treasure themselves above all else. They are trained to see their lack of happiness or lack of success—not their lack of righteousness—as the biggest problems in their lives. The attractional church does not create any desire for people to be delivered from their sin, because its message is predicated on the inner potential, not the inner immorality, of every person. You could walk away from the attractional church's pattern of teaching and think you needed some more skills, some more enthusiasm, and some more advice, but you'd rarely walk away thinking you need more grace.

And this is an odd thing to suppose, because the evangelical attractional church is big on grace. They talk about grace a lot. The entire system is in fact supposed to be the outworking of grace in response to the legalistic, traditional, fundamentalist generation before it. We can wear jeans now! We can play rock music! We can show videos! We can drink coffee in church! We've got a fog machine and stage lights and a whole new perspective on how people come to Jesus.

But what if all of this is neither good nor bad, but just kind of beside the point? What if applying the notion of grace this way actually cheapens it?

How would you know?

Waking Up in the Pigsty

In Luke 15:17, we read that the prodigal son "came to himself" in the middle of the pigsty, which was both a literal and metaphorical

---

[2] Ibid.

reminder of the wreckage of his wasteful ways. Some translations say he "came to his senses." The depths of his failure, his incompetence, and most of all, his sin, were now vividly before him, and he knew he was drowning. In the world of addiction recovery, they'd say he had hit rock bottom. The lost son could look around, take stock of his life, and realize that everything he'd trusted for happiness and success had not worked.

What would a prodigal church see if it came to its senses? How could they know they'd been wasting the Father's grace?

The prodigal church might see, first of all, that many people might be making "decisions," but the track record for growth in the faith over time was not as successful.

The prodigal church might see that, for all its talk of grace, most of its messages were centered on "things to do," which is law, not "things Christ has done," which is gospel.

The prodigal church might see that it might be appealing to people's pride by always talking up their great potential and capacity for greatness, that it might be appealing to people's greed in frequently giving away prizes at events, that it might be appealing to people's consumer idols by trying to fashion as many culturally relevant "experiences" as possible, that it might be appealing to people's inner self-righteousness by crafting a worship service around stylistic preferences and cultural appetites.

The prodigal church might see that it was cheapening grace by singing songs about how we feel rather than about who God is.

The prodigal church might see that it was cheapening grace by tacking on a gospel invitation to the end of an instructional sermon.

The prodigal church might see that it was cheapening grace by downplaying sin (because grace exists for sin).

The prodigal church might see that it was cheapening grace by expecting very little of people under the assumption that grace is an all-permitting grin.

Of course, the lost son might never have seen any of his failures as ruination. You and I probably know plenty of people who seem perfectly content, even if they are not happy, to stay in whatever miserable situation they find themselves in. Why do they do that? Maybe because they don't think it's all that bad. But maybe sometimes because the prospect of change seems so terribly daunting. The pain of change seems too great. And as a wise man once said, no one changes until the pain of change is seen as lesser than the pain of staying the same. People have to really, actually get so fed up with where they are, that they will decide that any pain is bearable if it gets them out of it.

I think many in the attractional church don't see the problem with their paradigm primarily because it has all the appearances of great success. The numbers accumulate, the buildings grow, the campuses multiply, the popularity surges. What's to argue with? Hopefully, you've seen that there's quite a bit to argue with. Appearances don't tell the whole story.

But suppose someone in one of these churches does in some way "come to their senses" and realize that things can look successful and not be, that ends don't justify means, that leveraging the spirit of the age for Christian ministry is not wise. Such a person may resist making any changes or seeking any corrections because the task seems too difficult.

When a megachurch from my past was going through a particularly grueling "train wreck" after firing their pastor, I remember speaking with the pastor of another local megachurch who had been approached by my former church's elders about pastoring both churches or maybe leading a merger between the two. He said he was flattered by the prospect and could see some potential there but in the end decided to turn them down. He said, "Changing a big church takes too long. It's like trying to turn a cruise ship."

We know that cruise liners don't turn on a dime. Neither does the attractional machine. There is too much at stake. Not just people and money and buildings, but an entire history of sold-out, all-in, guns-blazing allegiance to the model itself. This is why attractional church guys tend to insulate themselves from criticism or get reflexively self-defensive about it. You aren't just questioning their model, their way of "doing church." You are questioning what they've staked their entire lives and ministries on.

So it is hard for the attractional church to "come to itself." But some in the movement do. (We'll sample a few of their stories in the next chapter.) And when one has tasted and seen that the gospel is too good to obscure with the idols of the age and ornaments of the culture, the pain of change is seen as better than the pain of staying the same.

And the good news of God's grace is this: We can always start over. He does give second chances. He says to us what he says to the rich young ruler: "sell everything." If we are willing to abandon our deeply cherished religious enterprises and increasing platforms and burgeoning influence and multiplying organizations *for his sake*, we will find real life. He will come running to us, arms open, and bring us into a new life and ministry that is beyond all compare.

All of Ministry Is Repentance

The prodigal son comes running home. The father goes running to meet him. It is a beautiful picture of the repentance and forgiveness that make up reconciliation. And the whole thing began with the son basically saying to his dad, "I know better than you. Give me what is mine that I might use it now, however I would like." And the father was willing to let the son learn the hard lesson of doing things on his own.

Every day in ministry (and life), you and I wake up to new mercies. They are laid out fresh for us by our Father like the new day's school clothes or a morning-made sack lunch. He hands us a fresh helping of grace at each get-up time, enough for anything we may face.

So we take these mercies up. He places them in the open hands of our faith, and says, "This is for you." And we then have a choice. Every day, and every moment in every day. We may say, "I trust you, Father, for these mercies; give me wisdom to know how to use them." Or we may say, "Give me today's mercies, Father, and I will see you again tomorrow morning." And then we go throughout our day, presuming upon his grace, exploiting it, using it up.

Now, the reality is, all of us are trying to outspend God, and none of us can. There is more mercy in him than there is sin in us. So the point isn't that we can or should ration out the grace dispensed to us. The point is that there is a way to be mindful of this costly abundance and a way to hold it cheap by turning it into the "get out of judgment free" card.

So in ministry, we have a choice to make every day and in every decision we face that directs the content and substance of our churches. We can trust God for the grace he gives and work as if it is precious. Or we can presume upon God for this grace, distorting it—and him, in the process—by assuming that the reality of grace means license to do anything we think and feel.

Starting an Easter service with AC/DC's "Highway to Hell," for instance, is a cheapening of grace. I won't give more examples. Picking on people is not the point or purpose. Instead, we just have to see how prone we all are—attractional, traditional, missional, or whatever—to go off the rails and hold grace cheap. So every day we are tasked with taking up our crosses and dying to ourselves. And every day we get those new mercies. And every day we reconsider and recalibrate. Every day, we repent.

One of the hallmark cries of the Protestant Reformation is "semper reformanda," "always reforming." But this does not simply mean "always *changing*." The purpose of the Reformation then, and the purpose of gospel reformation now, is not some idealistic refining according to some upstart leader's new ideas, but rather a faithful returning to the truth of Christ and a reorienting around him.

The way we play with the shape of the church today arises from the worst kind of chronological snobbery—meaning, we assume both that the cultural context today is superior to the cultural context of yesterday, and that it actually ought to guide what we preach and teach. But the Spirit continually calls us back to the biblical portrait of the church and its gospel-centered parameters for ministry. I'm reminded of the *New York Times* story about the recent Japanese tsunami and its aftermath:

> The stone tablet has stood on this forested hillside since before they were born, but the villagers have faithfully obeyed the stark warning carved on its weathered face: "Do not build your homes below this point!"
>
> Residents say this injunction from their ancestors kept their tiny village of 11 households safely out of reach of the deadly tsunami last month that wiped out hundreds of miles of Japanese coast and rose to record heights near here. The waves stopped just 300 feet below the stone.
>
> "They knew the horrors of tsunamis, so they erected that stone to warn us," said Tamishige Kimura, 64, the village leader of Aneyoshi.
>
> Hundreds of so-called tsunami stones, some more than six centuries old, dot the coast of Japan, silent testimony to the past destruction that these lethal waves have frequented upon this earthquake-prone nation. But modern Japan, confident that advanced technology and higher seawalls would protect vulnerable areas, came to forget or ignore these ancient warnings, dooming it to repeat bitter experiences when the recent tsunami struck.[3]

Their ancestors knew what they were talking about. They had learned the hard way. And they erected markers: Don't build past this point. But we titans of ministerial industry are arrogant. We know better. We are smarter, more enlightened. And we have to

---

[3] Martin Fackler, "On Stones in Japan, Tsunami Warnings," *The New York Times* online (April 20, 2011), http://www.nytimes.com/2011/04/21/world/asia/21stones.html?_r=5&pagewanted=all&.

accommodate more and more people. So we ignore the markers. We want to grow!

But the biblical stones cry out: "Don't go further than this point."

Semper reformanda does not mean "always morphing." It does not mean that the church is ever changing, progressing into something better. In many respects, to be always reforming is to be always returning to the gospel. It is to be continually sloughing off the baggage of doctrinal add-ons and distractions, cutting out the ever-rising innovations, ecclesiological and otherwise. To be always reforming is to keep going back to the ancient markers in the face of constant temptation and taunting from those who would have us play with cultural relevancy ever-newly, who would have us take the grace given us and spend it like it's cheap.

Martin Luther's first thesis, of the famous "Ninety-five Theses" posted to the door of the Wittenberg church, was this: "All of life is repentance." If all of life is repentance, then all of ministry is too.

Paul says, "Follow the pattern of the sound words that you have heard from me, in the faith and love that are in Christ Jesus. By the Holy Spirit who dwells within us, guard the good deposit entrusted to you" (2 Tim. 1:13–14). He says, "Only let us hold true to what we have attained" (Phil. 3:16).

Let us return to the gospel, then. Let us abandon our visionary freedoms and run to the Father for his welcoming embrace.

Uncheapening Grace

When we take up our ministry crosses and die to our visionary selves and follow Christ's way of "doing church," we show how costly grace really is. We show how powerful it really is.

Ironically, however, the way to show the enormous costliness of grace is not to heap on people an enormous burden of instructions. The logical mind wouldn't think it should work this way, but you demonstrate how valuable grace is by emphasizing grace over the spiritual "to do" list. If you want to uncheapen grace, actually, you will throw it at everything.

If instead we treat grace like it's just for conversion, we hold it cheap. If we assume grace, we hold it cheap. If we "of course" grace, we hold it cheap.

The very nature of grace throws off all measurements of balance. You don't balance out law with grace, or vice versa. They don't keep each other in check. Thinking so reveals a misunderstanding of both. Trying to strike a balance between the two is to envision them as equal but opposite forces, as if they were synonymous with legalism and license. We think the way to balance away from legalism is to get some license in the picture and call it "grace." If we fear that "grace" is creating too much license, we seek to balance it out with a little law. But either option, to borrow from Lewis, who is borrowing from Luther, is "falling off the horse on the other side." Tim Keller writes,

> Christians typically identify two ways to respond to God: follow him and do his will, or reject him and do your own thing. Ultimately this is true, but there are actually *two ways to reject God* that must be distinguished from one another. You can reject God by rejecting his law and living any way you see fit. And you can also reject God by embracing and obeying God's law so as to earn your salvation. The problem is that people in this last group—who reject the gospel in favor of moralism—*look* as if they are trying to do God's will. Consequently, there are not just two ways to respond to God but three: irreligion, religion, and the gospel.[4]

In reality, both irreligion and religion are fundamentally self-salvation projects. They are equally self-righteous, even though the former is predicated on being automatically righteous and the latter aims to earn righteousness. So there is no wisdom in seeking to balance "grace" and law in this way. (When Keller refers

---

[4] Timothy Keller, *Center Church: Doing Balanced, Gospel-Centered Ministry in Your City* (Grand Rapids, MI: Zondervan, 2012), 63.

to doing "balanced ministry" in his book, he doesn't mean to set gospel against law but to set the gospel as a third way, the *biblically harmonious* way.)

The parable of the prodigal son certainly shows us the two ways to reject the father—in the lost son's irreligion and the older brother's moralism. And one thing we notice about the prodigal son's repentant moment in the pigsty is that he rides the pendulum to the other side:

> But when he came to himself, he said, "How many of my father's hired servants have more than enough bread, but I perish here with hunger! I will arise and go to my father, and I will say to him, 'Father, I have sinned against heaven and before you. I am no longer worthy to be called your son. Treat me as one of your hired servants.'" (Luke 15:17–19)

He went where we all impulsively go to please the Father: to the law. He cannot fathom that, after spending all his Father's mercies, there will be any left. "I'll go work for my dad." And thus he shows how alike he is to his older brother, who differs from him only in that he's been trusting in his works all along. The lost son wants to trade in his penitence for the merit system. He wants to trade the leaven of Herod for the leaven of the Pharisees. When navigating this divide ourselves, we note once again the wisdom of Martin Luther, as passed on to us by C. S. Lewis:

> For my own part I hate and distrust reactions not only in religion but in everything. Luther surely spoke very good sense when he compared humanity to a drunkard who, after falling off his horse on the right, falls off it next time on the left.[5]

That's not just a reaction; it's an overreaction. And it's where the lost son instinctively goes—falling off the horse on the other side. But that's not the way to find grace.

---

[5] C. S. Lewis, "The World's Last Night," in *"The World's Last Night and Other Essays* (Orlando: Harcourt, 1987), 94.

In many attractional churches, they talk up grace but actually preach law (advice), which shows how cheaply they hold grace. But in the New Testament, you never find applicational exhortation disconnected from gospel proclamation. For the New Testament authors, especially Paul, the practical matters of the faith are inseparable from the explicit emphasis on the finished work of Christ. Paul begins every message with an extended gospel presentation. The longer the letter, the longer the gospel foundation. See, for example, the first ten chapters of Romans, and the first couple of chapters of Galatians, Ephesians, Philippians, and Colossians.

Paul even bookends his letters with gospel proclamation. Every one of his epistles begins with some form of the greeting "Grace to you" and ends with some form of "Grace with you." When we begin reading one of Paul's Spirit-breathed letters, we should realize that grace is coming to us through the words of Scripture; and when we are done reading, we should realize that we have just received a divine grace in receiving God's Word. But this opening and closing reveals this theological truth as well: all of the Christian life is of grace. It is grace that saves us, grace that sustains us, and grace that will lead us home to heaven.

So when we preach steps and tips but only assume grace, we are withholding from people the actual power they need to experience God's love and obey him.

Grace is what makes Christianity unique among all world religions and philosophies. Only the Christian faith has grace. No human would have made this up. We love our merit badges too much. None of us would have come up with the concept of divine unmerited favor. None of us would have invented the notion that we cannot be good enough or smart enough, that we could not become somehow gods ourselves. We would be too busy building our own Babel towers, monuments to our own personal awesomeness. Instead, this alien thought comes down from the heavens, delivered by the one true God: that salvation is by grace alone through faith alone in Christ alone to the glory of God alone. Therefore, when we assume or obscure or otherwise deemphasize grace while at the same time emphasizing "practical application," we de-Christianize our Christianity. Thomas Smith offers a personal illustration:

> Several years ago I was invited to speak with several other preachers at a summer family conference. One of my colleagues spoke each night on the Christian family. What became more striking with each installment in this series was there was nothing distinctively Christian about any of it! We were given, night after night, good advice, sound wisdom, entertaining anecdotes, but we were not told what made the Christian family unique and distinctive from, say, a pious Jewish or Muslim family. This example could be repeated infinitely on a large variety of subjects.
>
> One of the most remarkable things about the New Testament is the way that its writers deal with thorny ethical issues. *Every ethical requirement, every matter of conduct, is rooted in the redemptive accomplishment of Jesus Christ.*[6]

So Paul says, "I decided to know nothing among you except Jesus Christ and him crucified" (1 Cor. 2:2). If Christ alone saves, if Christ alone is worthy, if Christ alone is the power and source of all blessing and treasure, why do we highlight application as some sort of graduation from the conversion experience? We don't begin by the Spirit and continue by the flesh (Gal. 3:3). We are not followers of Christ-*and-something-else*-ianity.

We can uncheapen grace when we open up the treasure chest of the Scriptures and start handing out Christ. It is from his fullness that we receive grace upon grace (John 1:16).

The Parable Continued

Once upon a time, there was a church that loved God and loved people but had a difficult time showing it because the image they

---

[6] Thomas N. Smith, "Keeping the Main Thing the Main Thing: Preaching Christ as the Focus of All Reformation," in John H. Armstrong, ed., *Reforming Pastoral Ministry* (Wheaton, IL: Crossway, 2001), 109. Emphasis original.

gave of God was rather one-dimensional and so the way they attempted to love people was also one-dimensional. The church believed in a holy God, a just God, a vengeful God, so they preached wrath very well, pushing the hearts of all who darkened the church doors with the imminent foreboding of their eternal damnation.

They did their best to scare the hell out of people, and when that didn't work, they cried and pleaded and begged. Wretchedly urgent, the church regularly reminded its people of the dire importance of obedience to God, of being holy as God is holy. And the church grew vividly aware year in and year out of the "thou shalt nots" of the Bible. And they came back for more, because guilt can be a powerful motivator.

But guilt is not a very *enduring* motivator, so as time went on and people grew weary of the burden of the law laid so heavily upon them, they began to drift away. Some had begun to suspect this church's god was not quite love and that this god could never quite be pleased, so they stopped trying. But some kept trying, of course, fearful and diminished.

One day some brave soul gently suggested that the old way wasn't working. People could not be won by a god who seemed angry all the time, he reasoned, and in fact it made no sense to expect people to be interested in a god who didn't seem to care about their happiness. The god of the old way seemed so preoccupied with holy things that he didn't care much for people's everyday lives. "Couldn't we make the way of the church more practical, more appealing?" this person said. "The way we may see growth again," he reasoned, "is to deconstruct the old way, remove the old barriers, and reassert that God is love."

So, where once the church emphasized God's perfect holiness, now they emphasized his abundant love. Where once the church emphasized obedience, now they emphasized success. Where once the church emphasized sin, they now emphasized happiness.

Where once the church focused on God's demands, they now emphasized man's specialness and abilities. "If we help people tap into their inner potential and remind them of how wonderful they are," the church decided, "and if we highlight how God loves them no matter what, people will be interested in church again."

They changed the songs, the architecture, the style of dress. They took the crosses down, because they seemed too religious. It was a clean slate. And, lo and behold, people began to come to church again.

The church grew in attendance week by week and year by year. People came excited and exuberant. This was not their grandfather's church!

But as the years went by, the church noticed something. Little by little, they discovered that while some new people were discovering church for the first time, most who came to experience the new way of doing church were actually in recovery from the old way of doing church. And while helping wounded people recover is not a bad thing at all, the church began to discover that most of their people—new Christians and "old" Christians alike—were not growing very deep in their faith. The lack, it seemed to them, was of a more relevant way to apply their faith to everyday life.

So the church came up with some new ideas to help people grow. They changed traditional Sunday school to innovative small groups, outdated special music to contemporary video montages. In order to help people see God's Word in the world around them, they began applying Bible verses to songs on the radio and movies at the theater. The church continued deconstructing more things, making more things over. The church had—in their own estimation, cleverly—traded out the don'ts for dos, but in the end they discovered that even the regular dispensing of practical helps for victorious living wasn't having the desired effect. People certainly enjoyed the weekend experience now. But day by day, they still seemed no closer to God than in that old way of doing church. In fact, though it scared them to admit it, people actually seemed *less* interested in God than before.

The church was not sure what to do with this information. One day the church's leaders sat around a table in the conference room and tried getting through a staff meeting without acknowledging the discouragement they all were feeling. They avoided assigning blame, they avoided casting aspersions, but mostly they just avoided the obvious problem: the system wasn't working.

It had worked at building a big church. It had worked at building an active church. It had succeeded in a lot of things, but not in many things the Bible actually called them to do.

Inside, each leader was yearning to break the silence. As they discussed plans for the week and the upcoming sermon series, as they reported on budgets and previous meetings, they each fought the urge to stand up and shout, "We're broken!"

It took the closing prayer. The pastor prayed a short prayer, but one that asked God for courage. It was what it took. Because when he said, "Amen," before anyone stood to leave, the associate pastor bravely spoke up and said, "I don't think I can do this anymore."

And as he unraveled, so did several of the others. It was scary and heavy but exhilarating. They all had a profound sense of something big taking place, something bigger than the ministry vision with which they'd planted the church.

It was the beginning of a very difficult, grueling, painful process. It was the beginning of running home.

10

A Portrait of the Author as a Young Man

I want to close the book with my personal story. I don't know that it will convince you of anything. But if you've read this far, I am inclined to say that you have earned my trust.

I want to share my story not to manipulate or convince you. The first nine chapters, with their appeal to statistics, cultural realities, biblical logic, and the holding up of the gospel were my efforts to convince. If that didn't do the job, I don't think my story will.

Instead, I hope that it will show you that this way of thinking is not simply a different model for me. I have not set out to get you to cut contemporary stuff and adopt traditional stuff. I don't really care about that, and I think we all should probably care less about that stuff in our churches than we currently do. I have set out to get you to rethink some assumptions, to question functional ideologies. And in this chapter, I want to reveal that my motivation is not the latest, greatest paradigm for "doing church," but *what happened to me*. What God did to me and for me.

I know a lot of people are jumping on the "gospel-centered"

bandwagon. I know the "young, restless, Reformed" movement has been growing. I have no interest in getting you to be a Calvinist or to join The Gospel Coalition. I find much more kinship today with Arminians who are passionate about the gospel than I do with Calvinists who are more passionate about their Calvinism. Wherever you fall on the free-will/predestination spectrum is not my concern. I'm not trying to sell you a label. There's no offer, here at the end of this book, to join a club. There is my story, and an invitation to join the gospel renaissance that God is working by his Spirit in our current age—to bring extraordinary glory to the Son.

I tell you my story, my own prodigal tale of "coming to myself," because it magnifies God first of all. And secondly, because it is the best way I can think of to explain how gospel-centrality is not an academic subject to me, not a trend or the latest model. This attractional versus gospel stuff isn't just me shooting spitballs from the back of the class. It's how I found diamonds in the pigsty. The gospel is oxygen to me. And I am desperate without it. And so are you.

But first, a few other stories:

The Light Bulb Stories

I like to call these "light bulb stories." I don't want to presume to place these fellows in the pigsty. I'll own up to that myself. For these guys, it was more like that "waking up" in the boardroom from the prodigal church parable in the previous chapter. There is a growing sense of disillusionment and discontentment. At some point, it cannot be avoided. At some point, the need to be brave overtakes the pressure to "go along to get along." These guys opted out of the attractional machine in different ways and for different reasons. But their stories are similar in some striking ways. Maybe you will find some resonance here; or maybe you'll have some fair warning about what might happen at some staff meeting in your future.

This first anecdote speaks to the sheer difficulty of stepping out of the comfort of a system that had become like second nature. It comes from a former pastor of a church from my past:

Once upon a time, I was a conscientious, career driven, successful minister. Working on the staff of two mega-churches, I built a career that brought me to the point where speaking on stage and in front of a camera to more than 2000 people a week was normal. Creating new ministries and teaching hundreds of people in classes and ministries during the regular week, and countless one-on-ones over coffee was a piece of cake. I ran into a couple of problems, though. I couldn't escape the Voice inside of me that kept insisting that I was created to work in small, focused, and personal ways that freed people up to be who they had been designed to be.

I also had a predisposition for pleasing people and being intensely concerned with what they thought of me. Particularly those in "authority." The longer that I stayed in ministry, the more obvious one thing became. If my soul was going to survive, I would have to push past fear of taking a different route than the one I had grown to know. I made the decision to face the fear and pursue the dream that I've carried inside of me for years. I thought that at the crucial moment it would be different.

I thought that it would happen with a loud fanfare, a swell of emotional music, and quite possibly a dramatic yell where the camera moves to an overhead shot. It wasn't that way at all. I found that changing my life started with small, quiet decisions. I only said seven words.

"This does not work for me anymore."

I sat in a regular Monday meeting, the same type of Monday ministry meeting that I have sat in for 20 years. Four faux leather chairs forming a square. A squat coffee table in the middle. Square windows overlooking manicured lawns. Decoration in the Christian/casual/corporate vibe, where we do serious business in our flip flops and non-ironic tshirts.

For 20 years I had sat in these same offices, in the same megachurches, having the same conversations regarding numbers and participation and programs and organizational processes. Which volunteers are leading or not leading? Who's on board with The Vision? Who is not on board with The Vision? Things that I knew were helpful and fun and desired by the congregation. However, while I always had a title of Pastor, there was very little pastoral work being done. I was only ever evaluated or paid on the number of programs, and the number of butts in the seats of those programs. Programs that I knew from experience were not healing people. Processes and programs that were not changing lives, or turning people's hearts toward God. And I had to say the truth, because the prospect of my own soul collapsing under the repetitive weight of NO LIFE CHANGE finally overcame the paralyzing fear of losing my livelihood—of losing my whole identity. So I said the seven words. "This does not work for me anymore." And I did not die. What do you know about that?[1]

I know a lot about that, actually, and the startling reality is that you come to this point only when you begin to see you're actually dying by saying nothing. There comes a point where that uncertain future outside the system becomes far preferable to the stifling discouragement and pain found inside it. "This does not work for me anymore" is very reminiscent of my own phrase, whispered to my wife one Sunday morning when I'd had one Christless worship experience too many: "I can't do this anymore."

My friend Steve Benninger is a pastor in Ohio. His story of divergence from the attractional paradigm is less dramatic and more gradual, but it is still quite powerful and impressive. I once interviewed Steve for a blog series. Here is an excerpt from our conversation that speaks to the matter at hand:

Jared: You have a—in my opinion—rather extraordinary story of a "gospel renaissance" in your life that has affected your shepherding and church. Can you explain what that process

---

[1] Bill Todd, "My Story," Bill Todd Speaking blog (n.d.), http://billtoddspeaking.com/my-story/.

was like, for you personally and pastorally and then for your church?

Steve: Oh my. The last three years have been quite extraordinary. I would have to say that my personal gospel transformation arose out of a season of disenchantment in which I found myself questioning the ministry paradigm that had been deeply ingrained in me for two decades. The truth is that we were products of the Church Growth Movement—we read the books, attended the conferences, adopted the strategies, and revered the gurus. "Success" came to mean numbers (although we wouldn't have admitted it), so a functional pragmatism seeped into our leadership ethos.

By all accounts what we were doing was "working." The church grew steadily and we were starting to get noticed. We even published a discipleship manual for use by other churches who were looking to grow and disciple people like we were.

Then some cracks started to appear. An original member of our team grew restless and felt the need to leave us. Then a new hire didn't work out well. A few years later a second original team member departed. During that time we lost three key staff members within a few months, and that rattled the church some. Growth remained steady for a couple more years, but then for the first time in our history attendance started to level off as we neared our 20-year anniversary. Our senior pastor grew frustrated with all this, while also sensing a new direction forming in his heart. Restless, he too eventually decided to step aside. At that point the church voted me in to the Lead Pastor position. Within two years I was growing restless too, but not with my new role. I was becoming disenchanted with our ministry philosophy and what it seemed to be producing. Ironically, the first thing that began nagging my soul was my own thrill at having an extremely strong month of attendance and giving during the spring of 2007. I distinctly remember having the thought, "Steve, those numbers are making you a little bit too happy. Something's out of whack if positive statistics have that much impact on your joy level. This is not good." It actually scared me. Shortly thereafter, several of our daughter church planters began leaning on me to rethink our ministry paradigm, contending that the team members we had sent out with them were not spiritually mature. These guys had been reading [John] Piper and were taken by a God-centered orientation to life, salvation, and church. I resisted and counter-punched, pretty annoyed, but my knees were weakening. I began to look around at our people, especially at the young adults who had started out in the nursery twenty years prior and had gone through our entire church program. "Where is the love for Jesus?" I found myself wondering. "Where is the passion and devotion? They've gone around all the bases and taken everything we've offered, but something obviously didn't get transmitted."

Right about that time Willow Creek's REVEAL study came out, and I was intrigued. I flew to Chicago for a pastors forum to discuss the early findings. There I heard Bill Hybels basically apologize for promoting a ministry philosophy that he was shocked to find wasn't producing fully devoted followers of Jesus to the extent he thought it was. On the plane flying home I knew something was changing in me. However, while I sensed I was releasing a long-held ministry paradigm, I had no idea what new paradigm to embrace. Over the course of the next year I felt like the trapeze artist suspended in midair, having released one swing but finding nothing swinging towards him. Was there a safety net beneath me? I didn't know. It was unsettling and frightening. That was a season of many 2 AM conversations with God, pleading with Him to make sense of all this for me.

In the summer of 2009 I attended a local conference which included Dr. D. A. Carson on the speaker roster. The conference theme was Understanding the Emergent Church, but Carson's sessions emphasized understanding the Gospel of Christ. He recommended a particular talk of his that could be accessed online. I went home that night and listened to the talk, basically a lecture on 1 Corinthians 15. As I heard Carson speak of the gospel as being not just for nonbelievers but for Christians too, and being the message "of first importance," I experienced what I call a "gospel convulsion." My soul erupted within me. I don't remember if I had tears or not, but great joy filled my heart as I realized that the Lord was speaking to me in an unmistakable way. Right in that moment I felt the swing hit my hands and I grabbed it hard, knowing without a doubt that gospel-centeredness—whatever that might mean—was the direction God intended for me and for our church . . .

I began devouring everything I could find online about gospel-centered living and ministry, and that fall I taught our church all that I was discovering. From that moment until today, New Life has been on a gospel adventure that has been eye-opening for hundreds of people. Rediscovering the gospel is progressively reshaping much of what we believed about salvation, discipleship, community, church, and mission. I'm finding that as the gospel seed finds soft soil in the hearts of God's people, it sinks deep roots and begins bearing the fruit of faith, hope, and love in their lives. Truly the gospel is 'the power of God unto salvation to all who believe' and it is becoming more and more precious to our congregation. We are now in the process of re-planting the gospel of Christ in our community, and trusting the Lord of the Harvest to call people to Himself through it.[2]

Steve has a pretty big church and they do some pretty big things. New Life in Gahanna, Ohio, is one of the best examples I've seen of a megachurch doing megachurch things for the glory of God in the centering of the gospel. They are one of the not-so-high-profile examples of how centering on the gospel for a way of "doing church" and rejecting the attractional church's functional ideologies is not about whether you're big or little, contemporary or traditional. It's not about size and it's not about style. It's about letting the gospel direct the methods.

About five years ago, I came across a very encouraging first-

---

[2] Personal correspondence. Extended interview posted at http://thegospelcoalition.org/blogs/gospeldriven church/2012/04/30/gospel-renaissance-in-a-megachurch-pastors-i-admire-steve-benninger/.

person narrative of gospel renaissance by a pastor named Joe Coffey. Writing in the *Themelios* journal, Coffey elaborates on his "epiphany" (his word):

> Hudson Community Chapel is a suburban church in the Midwest that averages a little over three thousand people each weekend. We were ranked as one of the top one hundred fastest-growing churches in 2007. I think we have done some things well, and I don't think our growth was the result of preaching a prosperity gospel or appealing to the felt needs of people. But in the last year there have been some notable changes—and most of them have been in me.
>
> During a mission trip to India in 2006, I was having extended time with God. I had an epiphany. I do not think many original thoughts, so this got my attention. The epiphany was that the incarnation was not hard for Jesus. I am sure that I had preached differently in the past about the great kenosis when Jesus "made himself nothing, taking the form of a servant, being born in the likeness of men." But I suddenly realized that since Jesus still had an unbroken relationship with the Father, it was not all that difficult for him. The man who has God and nothing else has no less than the man who has God and everything. Jesus still had God, so it wasn't hard.
>
> But there was a second part to the epiphany. As Jesus approached the appointed hour, each passing moment became progressively more difficult because he knew he was going to lose God at the cross. When Jesus cried out, "My God, my God, why have you forsaken me?" the shock of separation was unimaginably intense. Jesus experienced absolute agony because God had been torn away from him. He experienced infinite pain because he was devoid of God, deprived of God, and truly had nothing at all. Seeing this, I held my breath, wondering if I had ever really understood the depth of the love of Jesus for me or the extent of his sacrifice. The reality of his suffering had never struck me quite like it did that morning. It was the beginning of a rediscovery of the Gospel.

At the end of the mission trip one of the team members gave me a CD of a sermon called "What Is the Gospel?" by Tim Keller. I put it on my desk and thought to myself, "If I don't know what the Gospel is by now, I am in sad shape . . ."

A couple of months went by and I finally picked up the Keller CD and listened to it as I drove. Before long, I found myself sitting alone in my car, fighting back the tears. Keller was connecting the dots: Christ's relationship with his Father was shattered so that mine might be made whole. I suddenly realized that I had undervalued the Gospel by treating it as merely the starting point of the Christian life, instead of as the all-encompassing source of truth and grace that empowers all of the Christian life . . .

It has been a year of great growth inside my soul. . . . There is an infection of idolatry in the core of my being where will-power is impotent and the only thing in the entire universe powerful enough to cure me is the blood of Christ.

To be specific, I have found it to be incredibly challenging to give up the belief system that has sustained me so long, one built on an initial forgiveness and then fed through a powerful combination of pride and fear. This pride stemmed from the performance of spiritual disciplines, pointed to the obvious signs of success (we were, after all, named in the fastest-growing one hundred churches!), and most of all was fueled by the approval of others. But fear may have been an even greater motivator: fear of being exposed as less than what people expect; fear of not being as smart, spiritual, or competent as I should be; fear of not measuring up; and fear of Luke 12:48, "to whom much was given . . . much will be required."

. . . The truth is I have existed as a pastor with gods in my closet. There were times when these gods sustained me. Giving them up has caused more death this year than I would like to admit. The closet is still not empty, but the death of these gods has made me ravenous. Without the Gospel as my source of security and significance, I would die. So as one who has vacillated between self-sufficiency and depression, Gospel-driven transformation is both liberating and terrifying . . .

Rediscovering the Gospel is an ongoing process. Our church is a big ship to turn. I would never attempt to turn it if the approval of others was as vital to me now as it was a year ago and if I hadn't been changed by love, by Good News. In the midst of news this good, there is no better place to be—even if I am rejected by some and even if attendance falls. As a sinner-pastor, I stand in dependence on grace to plant and water Gospel seeds, recognizing that God himself gives the growth.[3]

I deeply appreciate Pastor Coffey's vulnerability here. It shows both his humility and his confidence. And I think his story is similar to many, many others. And it is similar to many stories yet to be written.

I love his honesty. He doesn't say, "I had a gospel epiphany, so I changed my model of doing church, and everything's been awesome ever since." He uses words instead like "terrifying" and "difficult." He brings up the prospect of falling attendance and rejection. But he stands on something much firmer than numbers and stats. He stands on the sovereign favor of God himself. "I stand in dependence on grace," he says.

God is waking up his church. As the desolation of post-Christendom creeps across even the Bible Belt, many more churches will die. Some will consolidate. It is predicted the attractional megachurches will grow larger and more numerous. But whether around this or through it, the gospel of Jesus Christ will always do what it has always done, as it goes forth into the world, bearing fruit and growing (Col. 1:5–6).

There will be many more light bulb stories. The light of these gospel epiphanies will get brighter and brighter until the radiance of God's glory in Christ is undeniable, irrefutable, unavoidable. As

---

[3] Joe Coffey, "How a Mega-Church Is Rediscovering the Gospel," in *Themelios* 33/1 (May 2008), http://thegospelcoalition.org/themelios/article/how_a_mega-church_is_rediscovering_the_gospel.

in Acts 6:10, the world will not be able to cope when gospel wakefulness explodes in the attractional church.

My "Gospel Wakefulness" Story

I was in the fifth grade the first time I saw pornography. A schoolmate had brought his father's *Penthouse* magazine on the bus. I have forgotten a lot of pornography since then, but those images are still burned into my brain. This is part of the pernicious evil of pornography. You can't un-see the depravity that changes you.

It was a long time after that before I saw sexually explicit images again, but that one revelation was enough to stir lusts already present in my adolescent flesh. They offered a secret wisdom, a power, a gratification and satisfaction that my childhood heart thought might be the answer to my inner adequacies.

I grew up a very neurotic kid. Whether by personality or by conditioning, I'm not sure, although I suspect a little of both. I had a pronounced stutter since as far back as I can remember. I was a smart kid, was reading and writing earlier than most kids and better than most kids. But I did not want to read out loud in class, for fear of people thinking I was dumb. I remember certain insults sent my way, some intentionally hurtful, some not, but each of which stung deeply then and helped give further inward bent to my low self-esteem, timidity, and awkwardness. It was in the fifth grade, as well, that a girl at recess called me a "stuttering wimp." I was already self-conscious and ashamed of my stutter. To be thought a wimp, for a ten-year-old boy, was akin to a knife in the gut. That a *girl* would put the two words together made it all the more awful.

One way I learned to cope and manage my inner self-hate was to overcompensate in the area of approval. I was a decent athlete and was pretty funny too, both of which were pretty valuable commodities in the grade school ecosystem. I made good grades. I excelled especially in English classes and creative writing, contributing poetry and short stories to school newsletters and contests.

In church I especially tried to stand out. I was always a very conscientious kid, very self-critical and serious about the things of faith. Internally I was still a mess, and this sometimes came out in religious expression. I remember one worship service, in about the sixth grade, where I almost passed out. In my mind, it was from concentrating on "the Lord." I asked my mom afterwards what might have happened. She said it was probably just growing pains, adding that it happens to girls a lot. Naturally, I asked her if I was gay. She laughed and said, "No, you're not gay."

Nor did I think I was. I'd never wrestled with that kind of thing at all, but you can only have your masculinity questioned so many times as an adolescent kid, especially if you're a total emotional mess, and not at least think the worst.

Thinking the worst. I was really good at that. A natural cynic and pessimist, I balled up all my mess—my fear, my confusion, my defeat, my insecurity, everything—and put on whatever masks I could in any situation. I just wanted someone to know me and approve of me. I think that's what everyone wants, really. Deep down, the cry of every human heart is to be totally known and at the same time totally loved. If someone could know *all* your junk and not run away, but run *toward* you? That would be eternally liberating.

The masks served me well, but only compounded my internal loathing. In school, I fit in with no particular group. I was a good athlete but didn't play on any of the sports teams, so I wasn't a "jock." I made pretty good grades, but didn't take all AP classes, so I wasn't one of the brains. In my last two years of high school I was the president of the Christian club, but my leadership did not endear me to the student body association or anything like that. My group of friends were guys who didn't really fit into any expected peer groups either. On the surface, our lunch table looked like a Rainbow Coalition of sorts, with me, Eric (Hispanic), Charles (African American), Tam (Vietnamese), and Babar (Middle Eastern). This was no conscious effort to transcend race. We were just kind of thrust together by virtue of being refugees from our expected tribes. We were all soft-spoken, kinda dorky guys. Oddly enough, it was with those fellow rejects that I felt most "at home."

Some of my classmates would have described me as the class clown and others as the quiet, nerdy guy in the corner. I projected whatever image I needed to, to keep my real self under wraps.

Youth group was a disaster, but only because I was so good at it. I had friends. I was one of the "leaders." I knew my Bible, and was exceptionally good at being emotional in response to spiritual things. I was a role model. I became the guy my peers looked to for answers in Sunday school, the good Christian kid every parent wanted their daughter to date (but whom none of the daughters wanted to date—funny how that works!). Outside, I looked very well put together, despite being too skinny and too pimply to impress anyone whose approval I really valued at the time.

I got my hands on pornography only a couple of times in those days. This was before the Internet was widely used, and even after it took root in the family home, my own family didn't have a computer until my first year of college. But I had been able to get my hands on a few magazines and rent a few videos from the local rental place. I hated myself very much in those moments. I felt the Spirit's conviction. But I pressed forward. It was a terrible feeling. But thrilling at the same time, at least for a moment.

But even when I couldn't procure porn, I made it up in my head. My endless creativity and my bottomless lusts were a potent combination, and I had lived inside my head for a very, very long time, creating my own private world. As a little kid, I imagined frequently that I was a movie star. I also was a pro basketball player and a rock star. A triple threat. It was immature and awesome. But as I look back, I see how the need to be thought great was embedded in me from before I even knew what I was doing.

I still haven't worked out how lust plays a part in that, but I know it's about more than sex. It's about power. And control. And having someone desirable delight in me. That's what porn deceit-fully offered. That's what my uncontrollable lusts promised. But like all drugs, the high wears off, and you feel ashamed, but then you recover and try it again.

Again and again and again.

Then I met Becky. I was a junior in high school and she was in college. An older woman. She was (and is) the best person I ever met. Somehow I knew this when we started dating, although a lot of it just had to do with this amazing girl thinking I was amazing too.

Part of Becky's story is that she had never dated or kissed or anything. She had made a promise to God that if he would make it clear who the right man for her was, she would wait for him. She admits she was kind of surprised when she discerned some pimply-faced high school boy was the one. But we fell in love.

We dated for three years. We didn't know what we were doing but we sensed early on that we really were meant to be together. I don't even mean in the typical adolescence romantic sense. I felt called into ministry while in junior high. Despite all my internal wrestling with my identity and my soul, I always knew throughout high school that I was going to be a minister of some kind. And Becky wanted to be a minister's wife. We didn't discuss this, really. It just was. We assumed it.

Becky bought me that first computer, before we were married. I kept it in my room. I had AOL dial-up Internet. I found a universe of snail's pace pornography on there. The image I projected out-wardly was harder and harder to keep up, but I managed. Privately, I nurtured my sin more and more.

My first real crisis of faith came when I was working at a church and was desperate for a mentor—that approval thing kicking in, re-ally—and not only couldn't find a pastor who would take me under his wing, but couldn't find one who would give me the time of day. I was on staff, but couldn't get much time with my ministerial supe-riors. And this was not a small church, but it wasn't a megachurch either. Not only could I not find mentorship, but instead I found marginalization.

I began to get paranoid because it seemed like someone in the church or on the staff had it in for me, but I couldn't figure out why. A pastor would pass me in the hall. I'd say, "Hi," and he'd walk by in silence, saying nothing. I remember a silent auction I was running one night at a youth event, where the pastor was on the stage with me and barking orders at me under his breath. I had never before been spoken to like that by a pastor. It felt . . . violating. Only my ministry partner and I could hear it, and we kept exchanging glances like, "Is this really happening?"

One of the rites of passage of growing up into the ministry in our church was becoming licensed for gospel ministry. This is the stage before ordination (which typically occurs after one graduates from seminary), where a church will officially recognize that one of its young men has demonstrated a credible calling and giftedness for ministry. I was already on track to be licensed, something I really looked forward to as another mark of approval. Then the pastor who was leading that process was fired, and the new team shelved the idea.

At first I understood. They didn't know me. How could they lead a process to approve me? But after a period of time, of my serving there and gauging the support of many people who'd been in the church a long time and knew me, I began to wonder where I stood. I asked for a meeting with one of the pastors. I asked him about licensing. He began grilling me about my motivations. It was intense. I had hardly ever spoken to this guy, and now I felt like he was judging my heart. My stutter showed up. When I tried to speak, he would interrupt me. He shut it down quickly. I felt like I wanted to die.

I tried to get a meeting with the lead pastor, thinking I had offended him somehow or had done something in my role in the student ministry that had caused someone to complain about me. I couldn't figure out what it might be, but I wanted to know so that I could apologize and make it right. He would not meet with me.

None of this may sound like much to you, but these were some of the darkest days of my life. It made me unsure about much more than I was already unsure about. In the end, I decided that if this was what vocational ministry was like, I probably did not want any part of it. That was itself soul-crushing, because I had devoted so many years to believing God had called me to this work.

Then a gleam of light. Becky and I could not withstand the pain at our church anymore, so we left to attend a church plant begun by our previous youth pastor. Mike became my first real mentor in the ministry; he took me under his wing and gave me the role of youth pastor at the church. Becky and I blossomed, both in ministry and as a couple.

We experienced real community and real love. The church was in the throes of the seeker church movement at the time, and we all ate it up. Though I reject much of the methodology I promoted then, I do not for a minute resent or reject the heart of that movement, or at least *our* heart for the movement. We wanted lost people to come to Christ.

The church licensed me. I taught the youth and wrote dramas for the church. Becky sang. We were part of an incredible small group. We traveled to South Barrington to pay homage at Willow Creek.

I'm being sarcastic, but we loved every minute. We felt alive and called and excited and hopeful.

We carried all this hope and excitement into 1997, when we moved to Nashville, Tennessee, for Becky's job. And that's when the wheels came off again.

During the previous year, in Houston, I had not exactly stopped being a lustful idiot, but I had stopped trying to look at pornography. The part of my life that was missing before had been filled. I was distracted. But the sin was still there.

After we moved to Nashville, we struggled to find a church home. We kept comparing every visit to our previous church life. It wasn't fair to anyone. We had unreasonably high expectations. We also didn't visit a lot of likely quality church communities be cause we were sold on the attractional model and pretty much used the Willow Creek Association directory page to find churches. We eventually found one on the other side of town that we didn't hate.

We were sporadic attendees. We were not in any community groups. We knew no one. I had reached out to the youth pastor to see about volunteering, offering my previous experience as a sort of resume. We met for coffee, and he was awesome, but it was pretty clear, when I started going to the youth group events, that his previously established team was not really open to new members. Most nights, I ended up just kind of standing against the wall, awkward and self-conscious like some of the less cool kids I was supposed to be helping serve. I stopped going.

That church grew bigger and bigger, but without any real relationships, Becky and I spiritually shrunk smaller and smaller. I was using pornography quite often then, as I was working and going to college and she was working—and we barely saw each other.

The thing about any destructive habit, including and especially porn, is that what you do in private doesn't just stay between you and your mind. It has real effects on the people around you. My inner self could no longer be contained by my outer façade, and the cracks began to widen.

Over the next several years, I became a harder and harder person, more miserable, more demanding, more "shrunken" in spirit and heart. I was not leading my wife or caring for her or nurturing her. I was not loving her. To Becky's great credit, she gave me all those years to repent, pleading many times for me to change, at each point of which I would beg forgiveness and then turn back around and continue as before. But all the while that she was pouring forgiveness into me and I was sucking the life out of her, I became a harder person to live with and she realized she couldn't do it anymore. And further, she didn't *want* to do it anymore. She felt betrayed by God, and certainly by me. She had waited for God's man, and I had been nothing but a spiritual monster.

I never hit my wife. I never yelled at her. But those aren't the only kinds of abuse.

One morning, after nearly eight years of suffering, she woke up and decided she was done. She said that, even.

"I'm done."

"What do you mean?"

"I don't want to be married to you anymore. I don't love you."

"What do you mean?"

"What I just said. I don't love you."

I promised to change, but she'd heard it all before and was having none of it. And I, too, knew that this time was different. The previous times when my sin had blown up in my face as I saw Becky's sad face, I knew I could get some grace from her. But now I could see that I had used it all up.

Still, I promised to get help.

"That's great," she said. "But I don't care. You might change, you might not. But it's too late. I don't love you. And I never will."

It was not emotional. And that's what was so scary about it. It seemed so rational, so cold.

That was the beginning of the end of my private sins. I was completely undone by this moment. Over the next few months, drawing into a little over a year, I daily grappled with the reality that my wife not only didn't love me anymore—she actually hated me. And I had put her in that position. I had caused this.

Over that period of time, I was very aware that any day could be my last day married. She repeatedly asked me to leave or acted like she herself was going to leave. I am not exactly sure what prevented any of this from actually happening. The Holy Spirit, of course.

In any event, we lived like roommates for about a year. She

kept our master bedroom, and I slept in the guest bedroom. At night, I would go to sleep across from my daughters' rooms, hearing Michael Card's lullaby album *Sleep Sound in Jesus* playing on repeat from Macy's CD player. When I hear those songs today, they still take me right back to the pain and fear and depression of those days. I would lie awake at night and tremble at the thought of having to explain to my little girls that Daddy wasn't going to live here anymore.

What kept me tethered was a profound sense of understanding that *I* had made this situation. It was my fault. Whatever she felt, whatever she was doing, it was because of me.

I just unraveled. Even while pursuing repentance from my secret sins and seeking to love my wife sacrificially every day, I was still falling apart emotionally and spiritually. And even physically. I went in and out of periods of depression. Some days I felt nothing. One of the girls would be hurt or sad, and I'd just stare at her like nothing mattered. Other times the slightest little inconvenience would set off my tears.

It's hard to describe depression, and not all experiences are the same, of course. But in talking with people who've gone through various "dark nights of the soul," I find some common ground with the ideas of an internal heaviness and an external darkness. The only way I can describe it now is that, inside, I felt hollow and numb but at the same time very heavy, like filled with lead. (I know that sounds contradictory.) And on the outside, it was as if a dark cloud had settled over me. It was the most helpless, the most awful, the most desperate I had ever been.

This led me several times to contemplate how I might kill myself.

But I was very scared of dying. And of pain. In the end, what probably stopped me from suicide was being too scared. My insecurity sort of saved me in the end, that way. But I believed that if I had ruined Becky's life, and if I had been the daily constant reminder to her of the pain and anguish I had caused, I could finally and ultimately prove to her that I loved her by taking myself out of the world. In my hyper-emotional irrationality, that made total sense.

In those days, I was clinging to hope in Christ extra desperately. He was all I really had. I still had this weird idea that somewhere, somehow, God might be able to do something about all this. I figured my marriage was over. I mean, it really was already. But I had given up any hope that we would be reconciled. Becky had said she hated me enough times that I believed her. She did. Instead, I pressed further into God than I ever had. I listened for his voice with more attentiveness than ever before. I read the Bible for the first time like a starving man tearing into bread.

It's my conviction that God will not become your only hope until he becomes your only hope.

It was in the midst of those days that I had my life-defining moment. I was living in the guest bedroom, spending many evenings with my face in the floor, wetting the carpet with my tears, praying from my guts. Sometimes I just groaned. I was desperate for God. And one night, in the middle of my groaning, I heard the Spirit say to me, not audibly but clear as a bell, "I love you and I approve of you."

This changed *everything* for me. No, not my circumstances, of course. And it didn't suddenly make me happy about the wreck I'd made of my life. But as I lay there dying inside and clinging to Christ's cross like the world might give way around me, as I stewed in the pigsty of my hopes and dreams, the fetid ruins of my calling and my marriage and my other ambitions and aspirations, a gleam of light came through the suffocating thicket and imparted a divine and supernatural ecstasy to my soul.

"I love you and I approve of you."

Now, I know God was not saying he approved of what I had done. He did not approve of my sin. He was instead pronouncing that, in spite of my sin and apart from the utter hopelessness of my heart, he approved of me in the gospel of his son. I had a grace awakening. I "came to myself."

Of course, things around me didn't much change. Becky felt just as she did before, and I wasn't going to her pleading my new experience as any justification for her forgiveness. I gave up placing any burdens on her like that. I simply, day in and day out, sought to demonstrate real love for her. I really did love her, because now I was serving her and caring for her without any response or reciprocation. It might never come, I admitted to myself. But this was the right thing to do. I was moving with Spiritual energy. It was not my power, but God's grace.

I walked in gospel-wakened repentance for almost a year, and then one Friday morning, Becky finally said to me, "I want you out of the house."

I didn't plead my case, I didn't point to the fruit of my awakening. I just asked for two days. Mainly because I had no money and wanted to figure out where I was going to go. I was devastated, of course. But I had known this day might come, and had learned the very hard way that if I have the grace of God, that's truly everything I need.

Becky said I could have two days, but then I had to get out. Then she left for work.

In the next few hours I cried and yelled and worried. I called my dad to ask for money for an apartment.

Around lunch time, Becky called. Her voice sounded different. She said something like this: "I don't want you to leave. I know things are different; I know you've changed. I don't know what we're going to do, but let's figure something out."

Somewhere between leaving for work and leaving for lunch, she'd had her own moment of gospel wakefulness. When I ask her today what made the difference, she says she just realized that I had actually changed. I had proven it over enough time and in the face of enough rejection that she knew it was real—that she'd actually known that for a while, but was too angry to forgive me. At some point, though, her bitterness had reached its limit.

We had a lot of work to do. It would be too easy and too tidy a story to say everything was fantastic from that moment on. She had a lot of hurt to process, and we had to have a lot of patience with each other. But for the first time we were on the same page. Every marriage has its difficulties, hopefully not all as difficult as ours. But I have learned from our experience and from counseling plenty of couples in their own marriages since then, that when there is real repentance and real forgiveness and a real desire to love each other—sometimes you just have to start with the *desire to desire* to love—there's almost no stopping the beauty that results. The Devil hates a couple centered on the gospel. But the Spirit will empower them.

That was almost ten years ago. We are now in the best place we've ever been. Our marriage is sweeter, richer, more exciting, more passionate, more lovely. It is full of more glory. We are two sinners imperfectly stumbling about life together. But we are walking in the same direction for once. And the longer you walk together in the same direction, the closer you come together.

As we look back, we see what God was doing. I have a million regrets, and Becky has a few of her own. If I could go back in time, I would do almost everything differently. But what I meant for evil, God meant for good. We would not have the marriage we have today if we had not gone through that utter catastrophe. And I would not enjoy the grace of God as I do now, and more and more each day, if it were not for that moment of personal revival. It was my "Saul on the road to Damascus" vision. It was my prodigal son epiphany. I have tasted and seen that the Lord is good and most glorified in his gospel; it has ruined me for all other tastes.

It is the gospel of Jesus Christ that finally answered my insatiable craving for approval, for someone to know me completely and love me completely. Only God can do that. And he does. The gospel finally gave me the peace and stability I'd never really had. I had been laid hold of, apprehended, hijacked by the gospel.

You might now be wondering what any of this has to do with the attractional church, aside from the little biographical bits. It's more integral than that.

During the train wreck of our marriage, as I was trying to find answers from God, I pressed more deeply into my church experience. We were still attending that attractional church, more regularly now, and we'd even moved to live closer. I started participating in the guys' small group. I was kind of the odd man out, because they were all gamers—and I mean fantasy board games, not video games, although I think some of them did that too—and most of their meetings had something to do with games, which I wasn't interested in at all but was craving community enough to overlook.

We started reading Bonhoeffer's little book on community, *Life Together*, which I mentioned in chapter 8. There was a lot of comparison between what Bonhoeffer described in that book and what we were experiencing at church, which Bonhoeffer actually says you shouldn't do—saying it's wrong to keep taking the spiritual temperature of your church and wrong to constantly compare your ideal version of community with the community you actually have. I can't speak for the other guys, some of whom are still in that church, but for me, the contrast didn't make me resent my church so much as it simply made me more aware of what I was missing.

Bonhoeffer says he needs the gospel in his brother, and his brother needs the gospel in him. We meet each other in the church as bringers of the gospel. It wasn't an ideal, perfect community I wanted. If anything, what I really wanted was a community that would own up to its imperfections! I wanted the gospel.

This became more clear as I got turned on to the podcast preaching of John Piper and Mark Driscoll. I didn't know someone could preach like them. It wasn't their styles, really. I liked the conversational, casual approach of our preacher. But the big difference is that they seemed to take the Scriptures very seriously. And through my experience, I had to. I had learned that my only hope and source of sustenance was in God's Word. So it became a painful experience week after week to attend a church service where we sang songs about ourselves and heard sermons that offered four or five or six steps to a better whatever.

I was so desperate for Jesus in those days, that I listened for him. Some sermons would go by without my even hearing Jesus's name. I am not exaggerating. I was listening for it. When Jesus was mentioned, it was often in an illustrative way or a quote, and in this sense he was used similarly to any other illustration or quote. He became *another* source, not *the* source.

During our difficulty, Becky and I tried meeting with the pastor at our church who was the appointed counselor. He was a great guy, and we liked him a lot. He was personable and easy to talk to. But there were a few serious problems. Whenever I talked about porn or whenever we tried to talk about any of the messier stuff in our marriage, he always found a way to change the subject. He seemed really uncomfortable with all the stuff we needed the most help with. He would always just go back to communication skills or practical stuff about gender roles, encouraging me to take the trash out without being asked. He said that a few times, actually, before I said, "You know, I have never forgotten to take the trash out. Becky has never had to ask me to do that. That is not our problem." It seemed he was wanting to deal with us in a more *Men Are from Mars, Women Are from Venus* kind of way. I don't remember any biblical advice; most of his counsel came from marriage manuals. I also found it odd that he never prayed with us.

After our reconciliation, we were both desperate for the grace we'd been changed by. We were in love with Jesus. And the longer we stayed at our church, the more we felt starved, as week after week we were sent home hungry. I didn't want to be the angry guy or the divisive guy. I was mostly the sad guy.

At some point, I began leading the church's young adult ministry, such as it was. I was preaching gospel centered expository sermons. Attendance shrunk.

One Sunday while attending the church service, I felt the straw break the camel's back. The sermon was about "imagining." If you just imagine stuff, you can get it. It was very much along the lines of the prosperity gospel. I turned to my wife and whispered those aforementioned words, "I can't do this anymore."

It was a hard thing, but a necessary thing. We had to leave.

Now, you may think this is just one anecdotal experience. If I'd never made a mess of my marriage, I'd never have been dissatisfied in my church. But this is not the way to look at it. I am not alone in my experience.

When my life fell apart, I had a notebook full of sermon outlines full of helpful tips and practical steps to being more victorious, happy, and successful. Not a single one worked. Only the grace of God was powerful enough to save me. I urge you not to deny your people their only help. They are inwardly (and some outwardly) crying out for help, for rescue, for redemption, for salvation. Don't throw them the anchor of the law.

Only the gospel works.

Conclusion

A Call to the Gospel Renaissance

"Give your ambitions to the Lord," Mark Dever says.[1]

I dared you in the beginning. I admit I played on your pride there. It would've gotten me. Maybe you chuckled and kept reading. Maybe you frowned. I don't know.

I don't want to dare you now. I just want to appeal to you.

If you treat your church like a business, you will see other churches as your competition. You will worry about turf and market share.

If, however, you can reject the leaven of Herod and of the Pharisees, you can experience the leaven of the kingdom. It is growing. It is expanding. The gospel really is power.

This is my manifesto. I'm not angry about it. I'm not throwing stones. I just want to raise the banner for the gospel. I want it to fly high over all of our churches, because in the end, they are not *our* churches, but Christ's.

When the end of the age comes, and the Lord calls us home, either by death or at his return, and we stand before him, we will not bring anything into his kingdom that we don't throw at his feet. Attendance, programs, buildings, campuses, conferences, book

---

[1] Mark Dever, *Nine Marks of a Healthy Church* (Wheaton, IL: Crossway, 2004), 247.

deals. If any of that is even deemed worthy to adorn the Savior, it will only serve as jewels in *his* crown, not ours.

The gospel is going into the world. It is bearing fruit and growing. The Lord is jealous for your involvement. The gospel renaissance comes Spiritually, and Spirit-filled men and women lay hold of it.

Recommended Reading

Dietrich Bonhoeffer, *Life Together* (New York: HarperOne, 2009).

Matt Chandler with Jared C. Wilson, *The Explicit Gospel* (Wheaton, IL: Crossway, 2014).

Matt Chandler, Josh Patterson, and Eric Geiger, *Creature of the Word: The Jesus-Centered Church* (Nashville: Broadman & Holman, 2012).

Edmund Clowney, *Preaching Christ in All of Scripture* (Wheaton, IL: Crossway, 2003).

Mike Cosper, *Rhythms of Grace: How the Church's Worship Tells the Story of the Gospel* (Wheaton, IL: Crossway, 2013).

Mark Dever, *Nine Marks of a Healthy Church* (Wheaton, IL: Crossway, 2004).

The ESV Gospel Transformation Bible (Wheaton, IL: Crossway, 2013).

Skye Jethani, *The Divine Commodity: Discovering a Faith beyond Consumer Christianity* (Grand Rapids, MI: Zondervan, 2009).

Timothy Keller, *Center Church: Doing Balanced, Gospel-Centered Ministry in Your City* (Grand Rapids, MI: Zondervan, 2012).

Colin Marshall and Tony Payne, *The Trellis and the Vine: The Ministry Mind-Shift That Changes Everything* (Kingsford, NSW, Australia: Matthias Media: 2009).

Ray C. Ortlund Jr., *The Gospel: How the Church Portrays the Beauty of Christ* (Wheaton, IL: Crossway, 2014).

John Piper, *Brothers, We Are Not Professionals: A Plea to Pastors for Radical Ministry*, updated and expanded ed. (Nashville: Broadman & Holman, 2013).

Thom S. Rainer and Eric Geiger, *Simple Church: Returning to God's Process for Making Disciples* (Nashville: Broadman & Holman, 2006).

Ed Stetzer and David Putnam, *Breaking the Missional Code: Your Church Can Become a Missionary in Your Community* (Nashville: Broadman & Holman, 2006).

Trevin Wax, *Gospel-Centered Teaching: Showing Christ in All the Scripture* (Nashville: Broadman & Holman, 2013).

Jared C. Wilson, *The Pastor's Justification: Applying the Work of Christ in Your Life and Ministry* (Wheaton, IL: Crossway, 2013).

General Index

"And Can It Be That I Should Gain?" (Wesley), 162

Ash, Christopher, 115

attractional church model, 20, 25–28, 84, 104, 178; approach of to missions and evangelism, 127; bloated attractional churches, 122, 127, 128, 132; and burnout of volunteers and staff, 43–45, 92; and church planting, 132–133; and church programming, 126–127; complexity of, 127, 128–129, 132–133; definition of, 25; the dominant message in attractional preaching, 27–28; focus on statistics, 151–152; the functional treatment of church as a place, 61; as primarily seeker-targeted, 63; primary aim of, 26, 104, 126–127; recasting of sin as problems, baggage, "issues," and brokenness, 28; rigidity of, 128, 133; "transfer growth" in, 35–37; the worship experience as event in, 59–60, 61–63, 101, 105, 127; and young adult ministry, 66–68. See also consumerism; megachurches; pragmatism

Barna Group 2009 survey on worldview among Christians, 74

Bible, the: as about Jesus, 77–80; and the Basic Instructions Before Leaving Earth mnemonic, 71; as God's Word, 72

biblical illiteracy, 76–77

Bonhoeffer, Dietrich, 69, 170, 177–178, 215

Boomers, 18

Breaking the Missional Code: Your Church Can Become a Missionary in Your Community (Stetzer and Putnam), 81–82

Capon, Robert Farrar, 85

Carson, D. A., 58, 131, 198–199

"celebrity Christianity," 28–29, 110

Chandler, Matt, 29, 66, 82, 118

charismatic renewal, 94

Christianity: as capital-S Spiritual, 53; as supernatural, 53, 162–168

church, the: biblical portrait of, 62; as community, 143; the early church, 68–69; the "virtual church," 115

church growth movement, 18, 25; and consumerism, 55

church marketing, 109–110

church planting, 132–133; and smaller churches, 42

church programming, 121–126; in the attractional church, 126–127; and the institutionalization of programs and ministries, 122–123. See also over-programming

Cole, Neil, 41–43

Communion, sacrament of, 47; methodology for, 49
community, and the pastor's weekly
teaching, 168–173
consumerism, 49, 54–61, 73, 104, 110–
111, 112, 124, 158; and competition in providing an experience,
57; and customization of product,
57–58; and the dictum "the customer is always right," 55–56; and
freedom of choice, 56–57
contextualization, of the gospel, 48
conversion, 163
core values, 159–161; and buzzwordism, 161
Cosper, Mike, 110
Cost of Discipleship, The (Bonhoeffer),
177–178
criticism, openness to, 173–174
Crouch, Paul, 29

Dawn, Marva, 113
Dever, Mark, 52, 163
discipleship, 144; the biblical blueprint
for (community), 170
*Divine Commodity, The: Discovering a
Faith beyond Consumer Christian-
ity* (Jethani), 59–60
Driscoll, Mark, 215

Edwards, Jonathan, 120, 150
eisegesis, 76
emerging (or emergent) church model,
18, 19, 126
excellence: as adorning the gospel
of God, 58; *Leadership Journal*
blog on, 159–161; the over-programmed church's struggle with,
134
exegesis, 76

fall, the, 172
Fall of the Evangelical Nation, The
(Wicker), 44–45
Finney, Charles, 147
Fore, William, 113

functional ideology, 48–49. *See also*
consumerism; pragmatism
Furtick, Steven, 29

Galli, Mark, 109–110
Geiger, Eric, 82, 129–130
Generation X, 18
Gere, Richard, 81
gospel, the, 70, 162–163; authentic
worship as about beholding the
gospel, 101–106; as capital-S Spiritual power, 163; contextualization
of, 48; as the essential message of
the Bible, 80, 85–90; the gospel
message as supernatural, 165; as
the "ministry of righteousness," 87
gospel-centered movement, 19
grace, 181, 181–182, 187–188; cheap
grace, 177–178, 182, 185; costly
grace, 177, 184–185; trying to
strike a balance between grace
and law, 185–186, 187; uncheap-
ening of grace, 184–188
Graham, Billy, 28
Great Awakening, 120
Groeschel, Craig, 29, 125–126

Harper, Ben, 33
Hawkins, Greg, 141
Hebrews, book of, 78; recurring phrase
in ("once for all"), 86
Hinn, Benny, 29
Holy Spirit, 162; quenching of, 54,
116; work of, 53–54, 70, 82,
163–168
Hybels, Bill, 26–27, 54, 68, 141,
142–143, 198
Hybels, Lynne, 26–27

*Inside the Mind of Unchurched Harry
and Mary* (Strobel), 55
Isaiah, call and ministry of, 52

Jakes, T. D., 29
Jesus: the Bible as about Jesus, 77–80;
as the bread of life, 23–24; High

Priestly Prayer of, 172, Jesus's charge to Peter to "feed my sheep," 144–146; on real worship as worship in spirit and in truth, 98–99; sermon of on the road to Emmaus, 78, 79

Jesus Movement, 94

Jethani, Skye, 59–60

justification, 90

Keller, Tim, 29, 64–65, 89, 150, 185–186, 201

law, the, 86, 87; powerlessness of, 88; preaching of the law, 87–89; trying to strike a balance between law and grace, 185–186, 187

leaven: the leaven of Herod (worldliness), 23, 40, 186, 219; the leaven of the kingdom, 219; the leaven of the Pharisees (self-righteousness), 23, 40, 84, 186, 219; as a symbol for sin, 49

legalism, 19, 23, 83–84, 88, 88–89, 185

Lewis, C. S., 13, 68, 186

Life Together (Bonhoeffer), 170, 215

LifeChurch, 124–126

LifeWay Ministries, 42

"light bulb stories," 194: Bill Todd's, 195–196; Joe Coffey's, 200–202; Steve Benninger's, 196–199

Lord's Supper. *See* Communion, sacrament of

Luther, Martin, 13, 90, 184, 185, 186

Malphurs, Aubrey, 55

Marshall, Colin, 159

McLuhan, Marshall, 110

measuring the right things, 156–162

media and technology, uncritical use of in churches, 111–114. *See also* video venues

megachurches, 19, 31; and burnout of volunteers and staff in, 44–45; increase in the number and size of, 34–35; multiple genres or "experiences" in, 32; multiple services and campuses of, 32, 114

"Megachurches Today 2005" (Hartford Seminary), 34

ministry, as repentance, 181–184

Morgan, Tony, 123–124

Morgenthaler, Sally, 31–35, 103–104

Mormons, 151

Moses: call of, 97; the radiance of God's glory reflected off his face, 85–86; worshiping of God, 96

multisite church model, 25, 114, 118. *See also* video venues

music: hymns, 17; worship music, 17, 93–94, 100

National Congregations Study (2010), 30

neo-Reformed, 19; alternate names for, 19

"Ninety-five Theses" (Luther), 184

Noble, Perry, 29

Ortlund, Ray, 104

Osteen, Joel, 28, 151

over-programming: and the creation of an illusion of fruitfulness that may just be busyness, 134–135; as a detriment to single-mindedness in a community, 135; and the dilution of actual ministry effectiveness, 135; and the distancing of a church from the New Testament vision of the local church, 136; and the reduction of margin in the lives of church members, 136; as the result of unself-reflective reflex reactions and an inability to kill sacred cows, 136–137; and the risk of turning a church into a host of extracurricular activities, 135; and segmentation among ages, life stages, and affinities, 136; and the stifling of mission, 136; and struggles with the pursuit of excellence, 134

parable of the prodigal church, 9–11, 179, 188–191
parable of the prodigal son, 178–179, 181, 186
parable of the rich man and Lazarus, 105
parable of the sower and the seed, 51–52
parable of the talents, 156–157
pastoring hearts: and Jesus's "feed my sheep," 144–146; pastoring hearts means being present, 148–149; pastoring hearts means proclaiming the gospel, 149–151; pastoring hearts means resisting pragmatism, 147–148; pastoring hearts means seeking souls, not stats, 151–153; Paul's perspective on, 146–147, 148–149, 149–150, 151
pastors, contemporary professionalization of, 75
Patterson, Josh, 82
Paul: assigning of credit for results to God, 51; call of, 97; the gospel foundation of his letters, 187; on "outsiders" (visiting unbelievers), 63–64; on pastoral ministry, 146–147, 148–149, 149–150, 151; "vision statement" of, 131
Payne, Tony, 159
Peterson, Eugene, 126, 173
Piper, John, 29, 215
planning worship gatherings, "first principle," self-reflective questions to ask, 174–175, 176: does this element adorn the gospel? 176; does this element exalt God, or man? 176; is there support for this service element in the Scriptures? 175; is this element comprehensible to outsiders? 175; is this element edifying to believers? 175; is this element offensive, alienating, or marginalizing to

any section or subsection of the church body? 175
pragmatism, 49, 50–54, 60–61, 73, 104, 112, 116, 124, 147–148, 158; as anti-gospel, 53; the difference between pragmatism and practicality, 50; as legalistic, 53; utilitarian ethos of, 52
prayer, as acknowledged helplessness, 166
preaching: applicational preaching, 81–83; Christ-centered preaching, 78–80, 85–90; community and the pastor's weekly teaching, 168–173; expository preaching, 78, 79; "Jesus as the role model" message, 81; preaching of the law, 87–88; proclamational preaching, 81–83; as a supernatural act, 165
Proverbs, book of, 50
Purpose-Driven Church, The (Warren), 27
Putnam, David, 81–82

Rainer, Thom, 129–130
Real Genius, 118–119
Rediscovering Church: The Story and Vision of Willow Creek Community Church (Hybels and Hybels), 26–27, 68
revivalists (of the '50s, '60s, and '70s), 25
Roberts, Bill, 94

sacraments, the, consumeristic/sensationalistic approach to, 77
Saddleback Community Church, 18, 25
sanctification, 90
Schaeffer, Francis, 53
Schantz, Daniel, 160–161
Schwartz, Christian, 41–43
seeker church model, 18, 19, 25, 26–27, 63
self-feeding, 44, 142, 143, 144
self-righteousness, 23
semper reformanda, 182–183

Simple Church: Returning to God's Process for Making Disciples (Rainer and Geiger), 129–130
simple church model, 124–126; and church planting, 132–133; flexibility of, 128; the simple church as more nimble, 132–134; the simple church as simple, 126–128; and simplification of the vision, 128–131
Smith, Thomas, 188
Spurgeon, Charles, 152
Stanley, Andy, 64–65, 73, 78
Stetzer, Ed, 42, 81–82
Strobel, Lee, 55

theology, 97; contemporary dilution of in the church, 75; contemporary gulf between the work of theology and the life of the church, 76
Thumma, Scott, 31
Travis, Dave, 31
tsunami stones, 183

unbelievers, and the worship service, 63–66

valley of dry bones (Ezekiel 37), 39
video venues, 114–115; as assisting the idolization of and overreliance on preachers, 117–118; as not countercultural, 116; and reinforcement of the kind of pragmatism that quenches the Holy Spirit, 116; as un-incarnational, 115–116; and the video preacher's inability to embody the life-or-deathness of preaching, 117
Vineyard Church, 95
vision/mission/purpose statements, 129–131; Paul's "vision statement," 131

Warren, Rick, 27, 28, 130
Wax, Trevin, 64–65
Wesley, Charles, 162

"What Is the Gospel?" (Keller), 201
Whitefield, George, 120
Whitney, Donald, 162
Wicker, Christine, 44–45
Willow Creek Community Church, 18, 25, 45, 129; post-REVEAL, 140–143; REVEAL survey of, 37–38, 39
Wilson, Jared: creativity and innovation of in his attractional church ministry, 91–92; doubts about the attractional church, 92–93; membership numbers in the church he pastors, 40–41; personal ("gospel wakefulness") story of, 203–217; student ministry of, 139–140; unlearning of the applicational, topical approach to preaching, 71–72
"With My Own Two Hands" (Harper), 33
worldliness, 23
worship: authentic worship as about beholding the gospel, 101–106; authentic worship as worship of God, 58–59, 68, 96–101; and being seeker-mindful, not seeker-targeted, 63–66; biblical portrait of, 62; contemporary dilution of the understanding of worship, 75–76; how we worship shapes our worship, 108–111; what we behold, we become, 119; as witness, 31–32; the worship experience as event in the attractional church, 59–60, 61–63, 101, 105, 127
worship evangelism, 31–34
Worship Evangelism (Morgenthaler), 31–33
worship leaders, tips for, 106–108
worship music, 17, 93–94, 99–100, 106–108
Wright, N. T., 102

Xers, 18

youth ministry movement, 94

Scripture Index

Genesis

1:1	77

Exodus

34:5–8	96
34:6	96
34:7	96
34:9–14	96–97

Nehemiah

8	79
8:8	79
8:9	79

Psalms

29:2	99
96:9	99

Proverbs

16:9	51
29:11	16
29:18	131

Ecclesiastes

3:11	104

Isaiah

6	52
6:13	52
11:1	52
55:10–11	82

Ezekiel

37	39, 135
37:7–8	39

Malachi

2:5	102

Matthew

9:36	144
25:14–27	156–157

Mark

8	22, 23
8:15	13, 22

Luke

8:5–8	51–52
12:48	201
15:17	178, 179
15:17–19	186
16:10	157
16:31	105
24	78
24:27	78
24:32	79

John

1:16	188
3:27	167
3:30	101
4:1–42	98
4:23	98
6	52
21:15	144

Acts

2	68
2:37	69

2:41	29
2:42	69
2:42–47	69
2:47	69
6	149
6:10	203
17:28	167

Romans

1:16	89, 165
5:20	88
7	89
7:5	88
7:10	89
8	89
8:3	88
8:30	90
10:17	82
13:13	95

1 Corinthians

1:18	165
2:2	90, 131, 188
3:6	51, 152
10:23	114
14	63–64
14:22	64
14:23	64
15:3	83

2 Corinthians

1:14	153
1:16	149
1:20	78
2:3	148
3:1–3	146
3:3	149–150, 151
3:5	166
3:6	165
3:7–11	85–86
3:8	86
3:9	86–87
3:18	119, 165
6:11	149

Galatians

3:3	90, 188

4:20	149
5:9	23
5:11	84

Ephesians

3:7	165

Philippians

3:16	184

Colossians

1:5–6	202
1:29	167
2:14	86

1 Thessalonians

1:5	165
1:6	165
2:8	149

2 Timothy

1:13–14	184
3:16–17	72

Titus

2:11	165
2:11–12	89

Hebrews

4:12	72, 82
7:27	86
9:12, 26	86
10:10	86
12	101
12:25	101, 103
12:28	102

James

2:17	147

1 Peter

5:22	149

Revelation

4	100
4:8–11	99
22:21	77

Also Available from Jared Wilson